Who's That in the White House?

The Turbulent Years

1933 to 1969

FRANKLIN D.
ROOSEVELT

HARRY S
TRUMAN

DWIGHT D.
EISENHOWER

JOHN F.
KENNEDY

LYNDON B.
JOHNSON

by Rose Blue and Corinne J. Naden

RSVP
RAINTREE
STECK-VAUGHN
PUBLISHERS
The Steck-Vaughn Company

Austin, Texas

To the memory of Mary Lee Graeme and to Rose's mom,
two very gutsy ladies.

Published by Raintree Steck-Vaughn Publishers, an imprint of Steck-Vaughn Company

Publishing Director: Walter Kossmann
Project Manager: Lyda Guz
Editor: Shirley Shalit
Photo Editor: Margie Foster
Electronic Production: Scott Melcer
Consultant: Andrew Frank, University of Florida

Library of Congress Cataloging-in-Publication Data
Blue, Rose.
The turbulent years : F.D. Roosevelt to L. Johnson, 1933 to 1969 /
by Rose Blue and Corinne J. Naden.
p.   cm. — (Who's that in the White House?)
Includes bibliographical references (p.   ) and index.
Summary: Examines the lives and political careers of the presidents from
Franklin D. Roosevelt to Lyndon Johnson.
ISBN 0-8172-4304-6
1. Presidents — United States — Biography — Juvenile literature.   2. United States — Politics and government — 1933-1945 — Juvenile literature.   3. United States — Politics and government — 1945-1989 — Juvenile literature.   [1. Presidents.   2. United States — Politics and government — 1933-1945.   3. United States — Politics and government — 1945-1989.]
I. Naden, Corinne J.   II. Title.   III. Series: Blue, Rose. Who's that in the White House?
E176.1.B676   1998
973.91 — dc21   97-19104
                                                                                                  CIP   AC

Acknowledgments
The authors wish to thank Harold C. Vaughan of Fort Lee, New Jersey,
for his critical reading of the manuscript.
Photography credits: Cover White House photo; Title page (all) National Portrait Gallery, The Smithsonian Institution; p. 5 UPI/Bettmann; p. 6 UPI/Corbis-Bettmann; p. 8 National Portrait Gallery, The Smithsonian Institution; pp. 10, 11, 14 UPI/Corbis-Bettmann; p. 16 Corbis-Bettmann; p. 17 Brown Brothers; pp. 19, 20 UPI/Corbis-Bettmann; pp. 21, 23 The Bettmann Archive; p. 25 Culver Pictures; p. 26 UPI/Corbis-Bettmann; p. 30 National Portrait Gallery, The Smithsonian Institution; pp. 32, 33, 35, 36, 39, 41, 43 UPI/Corbis-Bettmann; p. 45 Courtesy Rutgers University Library; p. 46 National Portrait Gallery, The Smithsonian Institution; p. 48 Culver Pictures; p. 49 Corbis-Bettmann; p. 52 UPI/Corbis-Bettmann; p. 54 AP/Wide World Photos; p. 57 Culver Pictures; p. 59 © Al Hirschfeld/Margo Feiden Galleries Ltd.; p. 60 National Portrait Gallery, The Smithsonian Institution; p. 63 AP/Wide World Photos; p. 64 Corbis-Bettmann; pp. 66, 67, 68, 70, 73 UPI/Corbis-Bettmann; p. 76 National Portrait Gallery, The Smithsonian Institution; pp. 77, 80, 81 UPI/Corbis-Bettmann; p. 83 The Bettmann Archive; p. 85 UPI/Corbis-Bettmann.
Cartography: GeoSystems, Inc.

Printed and bound in the United States
1 2 3 4 5 6 7 8 9 0 LB 01 00 99 98 97

Contents

Depression and Wars—Both Hot and Cold

*T*he word "turbulent" describes a situation that is stormy, "turned upside down." And that certainly describes U.S. history from 1933 through 1969. Five men lived in the White House during those 37 years. In that short period, the history of the United States was profoundly changed through decisions made from the Oval Office.

Franklin D. Roosevelt led the country through the Great Depression and the even greater turmoil of World War II. Except for Washington, he had perhaps more influence on the nation than any other President. After Roosevelt's death, Harry Truman faced the horrendous question of whether to usher in the atomic age. His decision changed the world in many ways. General Dwight Eisenhower came home to a nation at peace only to become involved with war in Korea. John Kennedy entered the White House with glorious dreams, but he died too soon to prove that they could be realized. Lyndon Johnson, with his strong stand on long overdue civil rights, took the lid off the prejudices that had been bubbling since the Civil War. During Johnson's years, the country—almost unnoticed at first—began its long, slow slide into a ghastly war in faraway Vietnam. Instead of "black versus white," the struggle became "true American versus coward" or "true patriot versus Commie lover." If you weren't red, white, and blue, you were Red, or a Communist. It was a bitter time.

The turbulent era covered just 37 years, but the changes in the United States were almost too great to believe. In the early 1930s, Americans were so caught up in their own personal problems that few worried about the rest of the world. They were far more concerned with the Depression than with a little-known but threatening Nazi party in Germany. Sports and movies were of more interest than world affairs. The old New York Giants of baseball won the World Series in 1933, and a horse with the interesting name of Brokers Tip ran off with the Kentucky Derby. A film called *Cavalcade* took the Oscar for best picture. A loaf of bread cost eleven cents, and a man could buy a stylish but sturdy pair of shoes for five dollars. For those who could afford more, the car to own was a Buick. It might cost over $1,000, but it

Wall Street speculators who had lost everything in the Crash of 1929 often had to sell their valued possessions in order to live in the early 1930s.

could hit a speed of 28 miles per hour climbing a steep hill! As the country slowly worked out of the Great Depression, Americans began to feel pretty good about themselves. And, along the way, winning World War II didn't hurt either!

But by the end of the turbulent years, by 1969, that good feeling was slipping away. To be sure, some exciting things did happen during the sixties. The mop-haired Beatles were busy conquering the music world. Bell-bottom trousers and mini skirts were in. An American astronaut walked on the moon. Boxer Cassius Clay, later Muhammad Ali, "stung like a bee," and everybody was shaking to a new dance called the twist.

Yet none of these things could quite erase the pain of that decade. America was now a superpower locked in a so-called Cold War with the Soviet Union. The fear of the atomic bomb and nuclear destruction was very real. School kids all over the country practiced crawling under their desks in case the Russians attacked. Americans were shocked by the assassination of President John Kennedy in 1963. The shock waves struck again in 1969 with the murders of his brother Bobby and of civil rights leader Martin Luther King, Jr. Americans watched their TV sets in stunned silence as blacks and whites sat down together at lunch counters in segregated towns and cities, only to be "hosed down" by police. Violent protesters disrupted the 1968 Democratic Convention in Chicago, and bloody riots broke out on college campuses across the country.

What was happening to America, the land of calm and plenty? For one thing, many people were starting to ask why so many U.S. troops were being sent to far-off Vietnam. It might not officially be called war, but it began to look very much like war indeed. As more and more Americans died, Vietnam bitterly divided the country. As they had never done in such numbers, Americans began to question the government. Should the United

In Washington, D.C., antiwar demonstrators march two miles from the Lincoln Memorial to the Pentagon on October 21, 1967, to protest U.S. troops in Vietnam. The well-known baby doctor, Benjamin Spock, fourth from the right, links arms with Dagmar Wilson of the Women Strike for Peace, to his right.

States be involved at all? Was it unpatriotic to say no? Was it cowardly to refuse to go?

The "feeling good about ourselves" feeling of the 1950s was replaced by the counterculture of the 1960s. The calm and plenty of the postwar years was replaced by the shouts of new voices, the loudest being that of the so-called hippie generation. They protested simply by going their own way, by "dropping out" of the mainstream that held most Americans. These young people, who wore their hair long and their feet bare, staged great gatherings called "love ins," where they smoked and swayed to their own music that sang of forgotten dreams and uncertain futures. The hippie generation, perhaps more than anything else, epitomized the lost optimism of another time. The country grew more and more divided and bitter. On one side, people began to shout about bringing the soldiers home. The other side was represented by a headline in a Manchester, New Hampshire, newspaper. It warned "all peace marchers, hippies, beatniks, peaceniks, traitors, and Commies" to stay out!

These were difficult times for America. They were especially difficult for the men in the White House who tried to keep the country together through the turbulent years.

Chapter One

F.D. Roosevelt: Nothing to Fear

Franklin Delano Roosevelt (1933-1945)

*D*ateline: Washington, D.C., March 4, 1933. It was a sunny day in the nation's capital. A 51-year-old man, his paralyzed legs in braces, was making his inaugural speech as the thirty-second President of the United States. He spoke to a frightened people. Since 1929, the country had been gripped by a deepening depression. Thousands were out of work, thousands had lost their homes, their cars, their self-respect. Hordes of homeless men wandered the countryside willing to do anything to earn a few pennies. America's pride in itself, in its shining promise and glorious future was at an all-time low.

Franklin Delano Roosevelt faced the nation's problems head-on. In a strong, forceful voice, he declared that this was the time to "speak the truth, the whole truth, frankly and boldly. This great Nation will endure as it has endured, will revive and will prosper. so, first of all, let me assert my firm belief that *the only thing we have to fear is fear itself*—nameless, unreasoning, unjustified terror which paralyzes needed efforts to convert retreat into advance." Promising action to employ the hungry, to restore buying power and the value of personal property, Roosevelt asked for the support of the American people. And he got it. So began the slow, painful road back from the Great Depression to a new status as economic leader and superpower of the world. It was a magnificent achievement.

Who was this man who pulled off what seemed a miracle? Who was this thirty-second President of the United States?

8

For one thing, he was a Roosevelt. That meant being an aristocrat, wealthy, cultured, powerful. He was born at the family estate Hyde Park, in upstate New York, on January 30, 1882. The only son of James and Sara Delano Roosevelt, he was unnamed for seven weeks because his parents could not agree on what to call him. His father favored Isaac and his mother preferred Warren. Finally, they settled on Franklin Delano, for a great-uncle. The infant seemed born for politics. He was distantly related to three Presidents—U.S. Grant, Zachary Taylor, and Teddy Roosevelt, his fifth cousin. He was also a fifth cousin of his own wife, Eleanor, and a seventh cousin of England's Winston Churchill.

Franklin's father was a wealthy lawyer and financier. His mother was wealthy in her own right. A good deal younger than her husband, she tried hard to dominate her only child and opposed his eventual entry into politics. She was so forceful a personality that she made Franklin's wife miserable during the early years of their marriage.

Franklin's life pretty much followed that of the rich young aristocrat. When not at Hyde Park or the family summer home on Campobello Island, off the coast of New Brunswick, Canada, he traveled abroad with his parents. He was educated by private tutors until age 14 when he attended Groton, an elite preparatory school in Massachusetts, and finally, Harvard. His mother chose the decorations for his college room and made sure he associated with the "correct" friends. Roosevelt grew into a lean and handsome young man, over six feet tall, with a charming, easy personality.

Roosevelt was a good enough student to graduate from Harvard in three years, majoring in government and political history. He was secretary of the freshman glee club and captain of the boating team, but was too light to play football. That was his major college disappointment. By the time of his graduation, Roosevelt's father had died, leaving the young man

Eleanor Roosevelt in her satin wedding dress, March 17, 1905

independently wealthy. He attended Columbia Law School and was admitted to the bar in 1907.

When Roosevelt was 23 years old, he married his distant cousin, Anna Eleanor Roosevelt, 20. His mother, to say the least, was *not* happy, even though Eleanor already was a Roosevelt. Her father, Elliott, was the younger brother of President Theodore Roosevelt. An alcoholic, Elliott died in a sanitarium when Eleanor was still a young girl. Her mother had died a few years earlier. An only child, Eleanor was educated in private schools both home and abroad and grew up to be painfully shy, insecure, and generally considered unattractive. She was not at all the socialite that Franklin's mother perhaps would have preferred—if, indeed, she would have preferred anyone. Sara Roosevelt even took her son on a cruise to break up the engagement. However, this time, as later when he entered politics, Franklin stood up to his mother. He and Eleanor were married in New York City on March 17, 1905, with her uncle, the President, giving away the bride. Shy Eleanor's first years of marriage were miserable. She was completely dominated by her mother-in-law, who was convinced her precious son could have done better.

Franklin and Eleanor had five children who lived to adulthood—Anna, James, Elliott, Franklin junior, and John. The family led the life of the wealthy and privileged, including weekends at Hyde Park and holidays on Campobello Island. All this, of course, under the watchful eye of Mother Roosevelt. But life changed for the better—as far as Eleanor was concerned—when Franklin was talked into running for a seat in the New York Senate. The young Democrat won in an overwhelmingly Republican district. That took the Roosevelts to Albany and out of Sara's watchful eye. It also put Franklin into the eye of the public. He learned how to meet people, how to campaign, how to get his ideas across. In 1912, he was easily reelected.

When Woodrow Wilson ran for the presidency in 1912, Roosevelt was his ardent supporter. His reward was the post of assistant secretary of the navy. This thrilled the young man who had loved the sea since childhood. Roosevelt is, in fact, given much of the credit for preparing the U.S. Navy for World War I, and he himself gained great experience in the art of politics and persuasion. In 1920, he was nominated for the vice president's spot on the Democratic ticket with James M. Cox. They lost to Warren Harding, and Roosevelt went back to his law practice.

Even without politics, life wasn't so bad for the 39-year-old wealthy and handsome lawyer. He worked, shuttled between New York and Hyde Park, visited his sons at Groton, sailed in the waters around Campobello, and generally enjoyed himself. Then the roof caved in.

One day in August 1921, Roosevelt fell off his boat into the frigid waters around Campobello Island. The next day, after helping to fight a local forest fire, he plunged into the waters

Vice presidential candidate Roosevelt campaigning on the Democratic ticket in 1920 with Ohio Governor James M. Cox in Dayton.

again to cool off. Then he jogged home and spent some time reading his mail before taking off his wet bathing trunks. That night he had a chill and fever. Two days later he could not move his legs. Soon after, he was paralyzed from the waist down.

It took about 10 days for the dreadful diagnosis. Franklin Roosevelt had polio, then often called infantile paralysis. The Salk vaccine has nearly wiped out polio in the United States and elsewhere since 1952, but it is a most frightening disease. Especially at that time, it was likely that Roosevelt would never walk or stand again and possibly not even sit up. His charmed and beautiful life was over.

But no one told Roosevelt that. With courage, ambition, and the help of Eleanor, he began a three-year recovery period. His rigorous exercise brought strength back to his chest and arms. In time, he could sit up. By the following spring he began to use painful braces to stand, and he moved about the house in an armless wheelchair. He joked that his shoulders looked like a boxer's. He drove a manually operated automobile. When his wife challenged him to become more independent, he accepted the challenge and met it. He never, never gave in to pity, and in his battle with polio, Roosevelt grew as a person. He had won his own personal fight with fear and it gave him new depth. By 1924, he was swimming in the warm waters of Warm Springs, Georgia, where he could stand unaided. Although his lower limbs withered and he was never to stand or walk again without the aid of braces or crutches, Roosevelt made light of his disability. In fact, many Americans never realized how disabled he was, even when he was seen in person or in the newsreels.

It was during the period of Roosevelt's convalescence that Eleanor Roosevelt came into her own. She patiently nursed her husband and pushed and urged him back into an active life. The public appearances she made on his behalf helped her to overcome her painful shyness. The once "ugly duckling" became, in

Harry Truman's words, "the First Lady of the world." With the possible exception of Jacqueline Kennedy, no First Lady has been so admired and certainly no First Lady has been so loved. She took up the causes of social reform and concerned herself with those less fortunate. She spoke out for civil rights and resigned from the Daughters of the American Revolution in 1939 when black singer Marian Anderson was not allowed to perform in Washington's Constitution Hall, owned by the DAR.

After three years of hard work, Franklin Roosevelt was ready to begin one of the most remarkable political comebacks in U.S. history. In 1924, he went back to practicing law, and on June 26 he attended the Democratic Convention at Madison Square Garden in New York City. He was there to nominate New York's governor, Alfred E. Smith, for President.

Smith, whom Roosevelt called "the happy warrior," was not nominated at that convention, but FDR won the respect and admiration of Democrats everywhere. When Smith did get the nomination in 1928, he urged Roosevelt to run for governor. FDR refused but was nominated anyway.

The happy warrior lost the presidential election to Herbert Hoover, but Roosevelt squeaked into the governor's chair. He turned out to be a good governor. Deep into the Depression, he aided the unemployed by creating a relief administration for New York, made credit easier for farmers, and reduced the work week for women and children. During this period, he began what would become the symbol of his years in the White House—the fireside chat. In an informal, easy style, FDR delivered radio messages to New Yorkers, easing their fears and boosting their confidence.

The Republican-controlled New York legislature screamed at FDR's policies, but the people didn't. When he told them in his 1930 reelection campaign that he had some answers for the Depression, they believed him. He was reelected in a landslide and overnight became a leading candidate for President.

It wasn't so easy, however. His chief rivals were Smith and John Nance Garner, speaker of the House of Representatives from Texas. On the fourth ballot, Garner threw his votes to FDR, who in turn picked Garner as his running mate. For the first time in the nation's history, a presidential candidate accepted the nomination in person. At the Chicago convention, Roosevelt said that he was pledged to a "new deal for the American people."

At the time, no one picked up on the "new deal" phrase. In fact, from his early campaign speeches, it was obvious that the candidate had no clear idea of what the New Deal was either. He often contradicted himself as he campaigned from coast to coast. But in a speech delivered shortly before the election of 1932, he had his New Deal down pat. Now everyone took notice. Roosevelt declared that the "age of the robber baron was over." No more would a few hundred corporations control two-thirds of U.S. industry. Once in the White House, he would help the average American, whom he called the "forgotten man," and make economic organizations serve the people. He would, among other things, balance the budget, create public works projects to ease the Depression, use government funds to feed the needy, aid farmers, set up unemployment insurance, and—of all things—cut government spending! And, oh yes, he would repeal Prohibition. This was done with the Twenty-First Amendment on December 5, 1933; bathtub gin was out and legal alcoholic beverages were back in.

In the 1932 campaign, Roosevelt travels the country to gain the votes of working people. Here he shakes hands with a miner in Wheeling, West Virginia.

The unemployed and destitute in America loved him. As for the Republicans and incumbent President Herbert Hoover, Roosevelt might as well have suggested treason. Hoover was in deep trouble anyway and the Republicans were in deep gloom. The country was in the midst of its worst economic depression ever. As Roosevelt's campaign crowds grew larger and more enthusiastic, Hoover's grew smaller and more hostile. Like a boxer going down for the count, Hoover began to lash out wildly in his speeches. He warned that Roosevelt's economic policies were so bad that "grass would soon grow in the streets" of America's cities, and he came very close to suggesting that FDR was pushing the nation toward communism.

Through all the accusations, Roosevelt remained remarkably calm. Circumstances were in his favor anyway. As the election neared, the breadlines lengthened and more banks failed. Fifteen million Americans were now unemployed and lots more were merely hanging on. There was little enthusiasm for the Republican campaign slogan of "Play safe with Hoover." People flocked to the Roosevelt bandwagon and the Democrat's theme song of "Happy Days Are Here Again" rang out across the land. It still does each election year.

The votes poured in on November 8, 1932. Franklin Delano Roosevelt was elected to become the thirty-second President of the United States. He beat Hoover by 472 electoral votes to 59, took 42 of 48 states, and every major city but Philadelphia.

As he waited for Inauguration Day, the president-elect once again proved how calm he could be. While he was speaking at a reception in Florida that February, a would-be assassin shot at him. The shooter was Giuseppe Zangara, an unemployed bricklayer who said he hated everyone who was rich. Zangara killed the mayor of Chicago and wounded five others, but missed Roosevelt. Through the mayhem, FDR remained incredibly steady.

Roosevelt gave his inauguration speech in March 1933, the last time a President would take office in that month. Since

Justice Charles Hughes administers the oath of office to Roosevelt. To the right stand Roosevelt's son James and outgoing President Hoover.

then, all Presidents take office on January 20 following the November election. After reassuring the nation that "the only thing we have to fear is fear itself," he got down to work.

First, he closed all U.S. banks for four days, a "bank holiday" in order to restore public confidence and end the run on holdings. No U.S. gold, silver, or currency could be exported. Next, he called the Seventy-third Congress into a special session. It stayed there for 100 days. With perhaps more togetherness ever shown before or since, the President and the Congress brought about a nonviolent, bloodless American revolution. It was called the New Deal. No one had seen anything quite like it.

The amount of legislation that FDR and the Congress passed during that short period in 1933 is truly impressive. Among the most important were the Emergency Banking Act, which allowed the government to inspect bank records and reopen only those that were financially sound; the Civilian Conservation Corps, which put young men to work building dams, constructing parks, and planting forests; and the Federal Emergency Relief Act, which gave direct Depression relief to states and towns. Perhaps the most famous piece of legislation was the Tennessee Valley Authority Act, which created a government agency to improve navigation and control floods along the Tennessee River and its tributaries, to improve living standards of farmers, and to produce cheap electrical power in a seven-state area covering some 40,000 square miles. The TVA became a world model of what reforestation and conservation practices could accomplish.

Farmers in general were helped by the Agricultural Adjustment Administration and the Emergency Farm Mortgage Act.

The Civilian Conservation Corps (CCC) not only planted trees but also fought forest fires. This one was at Deadwood Creek in the Challis National Forest, Idaho, in 1937.

The sale of beer and wine became legal, bringing in tax revenue. The National Industrial Recovery Act, the crown jewel of Roosevelt's plan, set up codes for fair competition and practices in industry and created the Public Works Administration, which in turn created construction jobs for the unemployed. In addition, Roosevelt took the United States off the gold standard. Most countries at the time followed the gold standard, which meant that money in circulation had to be backed by an actual equivalent in gold. This, of course, limited the amount of money a government could issue. Roosevelt took the country off the gold standard to stimulate the economy. Although the move did not have the desired effect, the United States is still off the gold standard as are all the world's major nations.

By the end of the 100 days, Roosevelt, in one of his fireside chats, thanked U.S. citizens and the government for their unprecedented cooperation. By and large, the American public backed the bold actions of the new leader. There were, however, detractors who called Roosevelt "king" and claimed he was giving the country away.

Yet, there was no denying it. The 100 days were indeed impressive, a dazzling display of insight, cooperation, and goodwill rarely seen in the halls of government. However, probably

Roosevelt's greatest achievement during his first four years did not occur until August 1935. The historic Social Security Act was passed. Today, nearly all American citizens are still affected by it. It set up a system of benefits to aid people in their retirement years. It gave aid to dependent mothers and children, to the aged and the needy. In short, the government was now charged with giving its citizens some protection from the hazards of life.

Franklin Roosevelt was a showman, a man whose bold and confident actions inspired trust in the American people. He was also a skilled politician who could be ruthless in getting what he wanted. He was successful because he appealed to reasonable people in government to work together, and he was successful because he placed talented people in key posts, including the first woman to hold a Cabinet position. She was Frances Perkins, secretary of labor.

Election time, 1936, rolled around. The President faced Alfred M. Landon, governor of Kansas, who declared that he was "an oilman who never made a million." This election is noteworthy chiefly because it produced one of the biggest landslides in U.S. presidential election history. Alf Landon took only Maine and Vermont and lost by more than 11 million popular votes!

Even so, the Roosevelt honeymoon was over—at least in the eyes of the U.S. Supreme Court. For some months the Court had been busy declaring much of the New Deal legislation unconstitutional. The National Industrial Recovery Act, for example, was called illegal intervention in intrastate affairs. In fact, so many New Deal cases came before the Court that Roosevelt grew furious at what he called the Court's "nine old men." And finally he struck back, unwisely as it turned out. A bill was sponsored by Senator Joseph Robinson of Arkansas in 1937, known as the Court Packing Plan. It would have allowed the President to appoint a new justice whenever a sitting justice did not retire by the age of 70 plus six months. In time, of course, this would have given Roosevelt a majority of the people he wanted on the Supreme Court.

It was a rare Roosevelt blunder. Everybody was angry, including the President's own Democratic party. The bill died, but it made FDR seem like a dictator, just as his enemies claimed.

By the end of the 1930s, the New Deal was pretty much over. Because the Supreme Court had overturned many of his policies, the President had to redesign some and fight for the approval of others. Although most scholars credit the country's economic boost to prewar and wartime manufacturing, the New Deal was indeed a milestone in American politics. It introduced the idea of an economic safety net and the notion that government could change the domestic scene. Rather than ending the Depression, its success had more to do with introducing ways to prevent future economic catastrophes. Social Security, for example, was a long-term solution, not a "quick fix."

As the New Deal was ending, the President and other worried American leaders were casting nervous glances overseas. Adolf Hitler, head of the Nazi party in Germany, was building his Third Reich, which was what he called his government. He formed an alliance with Italy and Japan in 1936 and began taking over European countries. Britain and France did nothing, and Roosevelt said nothing. Perhaps with this policy of appeasement, Western leaders hoped that Hitler might be satisfied with small gains and leave the rest of the world alone. Whatever they thought, it didn't

German troops invading a Polish town in September 1939 meet little resistance. In this case the town had already been battered from repeated bombings by the Luftwaffe.

work. In 1939, Hitler marched into Poland. This time, Britain and France took notice and declared war. World War II had begun. It would eventually pit the Axis Powers—mainly Germany, Italy, and Japan—against the Allied Powers, including Great Britain, France, and later the U.S.S.R. and the United States. In terms of loss of life and destruction of property, it was the most devastating war in human history, involving nearly every country in the world. The number of those who died has been estimated as high as 60 million. The destruction and human misery cannot be counted. World War II changed the world forever. (See Some Major Events of World War II at the end of this chapter.)

When World War II began, the United States was not involved. Most Americans wanted to stay neutral. But with the small countries of Europe falling to the Axis Powers and America's greatest ally, Great Britain, in danger, Roosevelt had to do something. In 1940, he asked for an increase in U.S. airplane production. The first U.S. peacetime draft was started. FDR leased American destroyers to the British. But when election time 1940 came around, Roosevelt promised the American people that "your boys are not going to be sent into any foreign wars."

It was an easy election for FDR, even though his own party was split over whether he should run for a third term. This had never been done before! Roosevelt didn't care what anyone said. He beat the popular Wendell Willkie of Indiana by a hefty five million popular votes and 449 electoral votes to 82!

Women replaced men in the manufacture of arms and other wartime necessities even before the entry of the United States into World War II. Here women are constructing barrage balloons in 1941.

Despite his campaign promise, the President must have known that America's chances of staying out of World War II were slim at best. In January of 1941, he gave his Four Freedoms speech to Congress, saying that world order had to be founded on freedom of speech and worship and freedom from want and fear. In March his Lend Lease Act provided Britain and other Allies with military equipment and supplies. It authorized the President to aid any nation he thought vital to the United States and to accept payment in any way he thought satisfactory. In other words, a country could receive U.S. aid even if it couldn't pay in cash. In May, Roosevelt established the Office of Civil Defense and gave orders to start building a bomber fleet. In August, he met with Winston Churchill, Britain's prime minister, to conclude the Atlantic Charter, which looked toward the "final destruction of Nazi Germany."

Still, the United States stayed neutral—technically. American ships and airplanes, but not troops, were sent to the fighting, and the U.S. government forcefully condemned the actions of Germany and Japan. So the situation would remain until December 7, 1941. In a total surprise attack on a Sunday morning in Hawaii, Japanese carrier-based aircraft struck the U.S. Naval base at Pearl Harbor. Much of the U.S. Pacific Fleet was destroyed and more than 2,300 Americans died in just a few hours.

Shocked, angered, and frightened, Americans once again looked to the President for reassurance. This was surely one of Roosevelt's

Thick smoke rolls from a burning ship during the attack by the Japanese on Pearl Harbor, Hawaii, December 7, 1941. Shown here the battleships USS West Virginia *and USS* Tennessee.

finest hours. On Monday, December 8, 1941, his son James at his side, FDR slowly walked into the House of Representatives. In a confident and ringing voice, he declared that December 7 was "a date that will live in infamy....Always will we remember the character of the attack against us."

After a vote of Congress, the United States of America entered World War II. Only one member of the House of Representatives—Jeannette Rankin of Montana, a pacifist—voted against declaring war. More than 16 million Americans would serve in World War II, and more than 400,000 would die.

It is impossible to calculate what Roosevelt meant to the country during World War II. Although he did make military decisions, he did not personally direct the military effort, leaving that to such fine leaders as Admiral William Leahy and General George C. Marshall. He did not personally mobilize the power of U.S. industry. But he was there, his voice sure and strong, inspiring confidence, trust, and hope. This was not easy during the early years of the war when Germany was crushing Europe and island after island fell to Japan in the Pacific.

But perhaps FDR's greatest contribution to the war effort was his brilliance as a diplomat. His international conferences were historic and vastly important to the war's outcome. He met with Churchill in Casablanca in 1943 to combine British and American invasion plans. Both men warned the Axis that they would accept only "unconditional surrender." FDR met with the U.S.S.R.'s Joseph Stalin later in the year at Teheran. He promised a British-American invasion through France, if Stalin would promise to fight Japan once Germany was defeated. On December 6, 1944, the Allies launched their long-promised invasion of the European mainland. It is known as D-Day. General George Patton and his Third Army were soon driving inland. Paris was liberated to tumultuous celebration in August. From December 1944 to January 1945, the Germans made one last desperate stab at keeping the Allies out of their homeland. The unsuccessful attempt in the Ardennes Forest in southern Belgium was called the Battle of the Bulge. American troops pushed the enemy back, and now the end of the war was in sight.

In February 1945, at a conference in Yalta, on the Crimean Peninsula, FDR and Churchill met with Stalin to plan the final defeat and occupation of Nazi Germany. It is this Yalta Conference that drew the greatest criticism against FDR. Both Roosevelt and Churchill believed Stalin when he gave his word about holding free elections in the Soviet-held nations of Europe. They were not naive about the Soviet leader, but they—mistakenly as it turned out—believed that Russian troops would be essential to defeat Japan. And, although Roosevelt had okayed the building of the atomic bomb, it was not yet ready for use. So, Roosevelt and Churchill conceded a number of issues to Stalin, such as recognizing the Soviet "sphere of influence" in Europe.

When Stalin did not honor the agreements made at Yalta, Britain and the United States were powerless to stop the spread of communism in Europe. The concessions given to Stalin at Yalta helped bring about his rigid Communist regime in the U.S.S.R. and foster the Cold War. Criticism aside, Roosevelt did get something else he very much wanted at Yalta. The Allies agreed to hold a conference in San Francisco on April 25, 1945, to plan a peacetime United Nations organization.

With the end of this terrible war approaching, Roosevelt once more had to turn his attention to a national election. He ran for an unprecedented fourth term against the New York governor, Thomas E. Dewey. Since it was difficult to attack Roosevelt's foreign policy right in the middle of

During the Yalta Conference, in 1945, Churchill, Roosevelt, and Stalin (left to right) pose for this official photo.

World War II, Dewey, instead, attacked Roosevelt. He implied that the President was tired and in poor health. In the 1990s, such methods are called "negative campaigning." In response, Roosevelt campaigned in bad weather and trotted out his physician to say he was in good health. When Dewey declared that FDR and his administration were wasting the people's money, the Democrats hit back with their campaign slogan: "Don't change horses in the middle of the stream." The spending charges did, however, give the President a chance to show a little humor. The Republicans said Roosevelt had sent a Navy ship to get his pet dog, who had been left behind after the President was on an inspection tour. Roosevelt said in a speech following the incident that the opposition wasn't content with attacking him or his wife or his sons, "...now they include my little dog, Fala. Well, of course, I don't resent attacks, and my family doesn't resent attacks, but Fala does resent them."

Charges against Roosevelt of ill health and big spending didn't help Dewey into the White House. Franklin Roosevelt became the only U.S. President to win a fourth term. Yet, he was voted in by the slimmest margin of all four elections. He beat Dewey by about three million votes, and 432 electoral votes to 99.

It was a solemn inaugural address delivered on January 20, 1945, to a nation still at war. Said the President, "Today, in this year of war, 1945, we have learned lessons—at a fearful cost—and we shall profit by them."

Franklin Delano Roosevelt never lived to see the end of World War II or the opening of the United Nations conference. Unknown to the public, he had collapsed after his inaugural address, and when he attended the meeting at Yalta, for the first time as President, he remained seated.

In Warm Springs, Georgia, resting to get ready for the UN meeting, the President sat for his portrait on April 12, 1945. He complained of a headache and slumped in his chair. At 3:35 P.M., he died of a cerebral hemorrhage.

The nation was stunned. It had lost a leader, a commander in chief, and to many, a father figure. Harry S Truman was now President. Henry Wallace of Iowa had been Roosevelt's vice president for the third term. But party leaders decided he was too pro-Communist and persuaded FDR to drop him from the ticket for the 1944 election. Wallace was replaced with Truman of Missouri.

Millions of Americans mourned as FDR's funeral train slowly moved north from Georgia to Hyde Park, New York, where he was buried. Said Mrs. Roosevelt of her husband, "He might have been happier with a wife who was completely uncritical. That I was never able to be." The former First Lady continued to be active until her death in 1962. President Truman named her to the first U.S. delegation to the United Nations, and she was reappointed by President Kennedy in 1961.

Eleanor Roosevelt earned the deepening love and admiration of the American people. The "ugly duckling" had grown in dignity and graciousness throughout her public life. What the public saw was a genuinely caring person who took her role in the political spotlight most seriously. She ladled soup in a breadline during the Depression, visited soldiers in the Pacific during World War II, and tended the sick in city slums. Throughout the Roosevelt years in office, the First Lady seemed to be everywhere. She was affectionately kidded about it in a cartoon in the *New Yorker* magazine. It showed a soot-covered coal miner at work. He stops

Eleanor Roosevelt, who was very active during World War II arranging benefits for people in the armed services, presents the one-millionth free ticket to New York City entertainment from the city's Defense Recreation Committee to Corp. William Raney of Seattle.

shoveling and whispers to a coworker in amazement: "For gosh sakes, here comes Mrs. Roosevelt!"

As Eleanor Roosevelt was much loved and admired, so was Franklin. But the President had a legion of enemies as well. They called him a "Red lover," saying he had led the nation into war only to sell out to Stalin. They scorned his domestic policies, calling him traitor and dictator. But his admirers far outnumbered his detractors. They saw him as the man who saved capitalism, who was largely responsible for victory in World War II, who defended minorities and labor, and was a friend of the poor.

No matter how people saw him, no one could deny his impact on the world, the country, and the White House. He changed modern history. He shaped it by his strong will, by the force of his personal convictions, and the introduction of a radically new interventionist approach to government. He changed political alignments in the 1930s and created the modern Democratic party. Historian William S. White wrote at FDR's death that "...to a generation who had known no other president, it seemed, too, as if the presidency had died, as if the United States could not go on."

With the Capitol building in the background, Franklin Roosevelt's flag-draped casket on a horse-drawn caisson passes thousands of mourners on its way from Union Station to the White House.

Indeed, that was true. Many Americans born in the late 1920s or early 1930s were well into their teens before they realized that the United States did not have one permanent President. Elections came and went, but the outcome was always the same. Roosevelt was in the White House. That was that. FDR would always be there. In fact, after his death one of his Secret Service guards said almost in astonishment, "I never believed he'd die."

But he did, at the age of 63. FDR was President from 1932 until 1945, the longest of anyone who sat in the White House. And unless the Twenty-Second Amendment of 1951 is repealed, no one—man or woman—will ever occupy the White House longer.

It was a unique time. Roosevelt was a unique President. Almost surely, the two will never happen again.

Names in the News in Roosevelt's Time

Hugo L. Black (1886–1971):

Liberal Alabama lawyer; FDR's first appointee to the Supreme Court (1937), breaking Court's conservative monopoly; staunch defender of personal liberties.

Cordell Hull (1871–1955):

Born Tennessee; secretary of state (1933–1944); Nobel Peace Prize (1945).

Jesse Owens (1913–1980):

African American track and field star, born in Alabama; won four gold medals at 1936 Olympics in Berlin, infuriating Adolf Hitler.

Frances Perkins (1882–1965):

Boston-born, no-nonsense secretary of labor (1933–1945), first woman to hold a Cabinet post. When asked if being a woman would handicap her in that position, she replied, "Only in climbing trees."

John Steinbeck (1902–1968):

California-born Nobel winning novelist. Noted for *Tortilla Flat* (1935), *Of Mice and Men* (1937), *The Grapes of Wrath* (1939), *East of Eden* (1952).

Wendell L. Willkie (1892–1944):

Born Indiana; became New York attorney; lost to FDR in 1940 presidential election.

Some Major Events of World War II

1939	Sept. 1	Germany invades Poland.
	Sept. 3	Great Britain and France declare war on Germany.
1940	Apr. 9	Germany invades Norway and Denmark.
	May 15	Dutch Army surrenders to Germany.
	May 28	Belgian Army surrenders to Germany.
	June 4	Britain evacuates army at Dunkirk.
	June 10	Italy declares war on Britain and France.
	June 22/24	France signs armistice with Germany/Italy.
	July 10	Battle of Britain begins.
1941	May 27	Roosevelt declares national emergency.
	June 22	Germany invades U.S.S.R.; Italy declares war on U.S.S.R.
	Dec. 7	Japan attacks Pearl Harbor, Hawaii.
	Dec. 8	U.S. and Great Britain declare war on Japan.
	Dec. 11	Germany and Italy declare war on U.S.
	Dec. 14	Japan invades Burma.
	Dec. 24	Japan captures Wake Island.
1942	March 17	General Douglas MacArthur appointed to Southwest Pacific area.
	April 9	U.S. surrenders the Philippines at Bataan.
	April 18	Lt. Col. James Doolittle bombs Tokyo.
	May 6	Corregidor Island falls to Japan.
	May 7	Battle of Coral Sea
	June 4	Battle of Midway
	Aug. 7	U.S. troops land at Guadalcanal.
1943	March 2	Battle of Bismarck Sea
	May 24	Germany withdraws U-boats from Atlantic.
	July 25	Italy's dictator, Benito Mussolini, resigns.
	Sept. 3	Allies land in Italy.
	Sept. 8	Italy surrenders.
	Oct. 13	Italy declares war on Germany.
	Nov. 20	U.S. forces land on Pacific island of Tarawa.
	Dec. 2	Atomic bomb developed, first chain reaction of nuclear fusion achieved in Chicago.
	Dec. 24	General Dwight Eisenhower named Supreme Commander of the Allied Expeditionary Force in Western Europe.
1944	Jan. 4	Red Army crosses Polish border.
	Jan. 22	Allies land at Anzio.
	Jan. 27	German siege of Leningrad ends.
	Jan. 31	U.S. lands on Marshall Islands.
	Apr. 10	Red Army captures Odessa in the Ukraine.

	Apr. 22	MacArthur lands in New Guinea.
	June 4	U.S. troops enter Rome.
	June 6	D-Day. Allies land on the beaches of Normandy, France. Operation Overlord begins
	June 13	Germans start V-1 guided missile bombardment of England.
	June 19	Battle of the Philippine Sea
	July 18	Japan's leader, Tojo, resigns.
	July 20	Assassination attempt against Hitler fails.
	Aug. 25	Free French and American forces liberate Paris.
	Sept. 8	Red Army enters Bulgaria, which surrenders.
	Oct. 20	Allied troops land in the Philippines.
	Oct. 23–26	Allies defeat Japan in Battle of Leyte Gulf, Philippines.
1945	Jan. 17	Red Army takes Warsaw, Poland, advances into Germany.
	Jan. 8–16	Battle of the Bulge, last German major offensive thrust
	March 16	U.S. takes island of Iwo Jima in Pacific.
	April 30	Hitler commits suicide.
	May 8	Germany surrenders.
	June 21	Allied troops take Okinawa.
	Aug. 6/9	Atomic bombs dropped on Hiroshima and Nagasaki.
	Sept. 2	Japan formally surrenders; World War II ends.

Some American Military Leaders in World War II

Henry "Hap" Arnold (1886–1950): General, chief of U.S. air forces

Omar N. Bradley (1893–1981): General, commander, Tunisia, Europe

Dwight D. Eisenhower (1890–1969): See Chapter Three, pages 46-59.

William "Bull" Halsey (1882–1959): Admiral, commander Allied forces, South Pacific (1942–1944), U.S. 3rd fleet (1944–1945)

William Leahy (1875–1959): Admiral, FDR chief of staff (1942), admiral of the fleet (1944)

Douglas MacArthur (1880–1964): General, commander Army forces in the Far East (1941); commander Allied forces in the southwest Pacific (1942); general of the army (1944); Allied supreme commander (1945); commander occupation forces, Japan (1945–1951)

George C. Marshall (1880–1959): Chief of Staff, U.S. Army (1939–1945); general of the army (1944)

Chester W. Nimitz (1885–1966): Admiral, commander U.S. Pacific Fleet (1941–1945); chief of naval operations (1945–1947)

George S. Patton (1885–1945): General, commander 2nd Army Corps, Tunisia (1943), U.S. 7th Army, Sicily (1943), 3rd Army, Western Europe (1944–1945)

Chapter Two

Truman, the Bomb, and the Biggest Surprise

Harry S Truman (1945-1953)

*I*t was election day 1948. Conversations like the following were going on all over the country. *"Don't waste your vote on Truman, Charlie. The Republicans are in. It's Dewey all the way! You can bet the farm on it."*

"How come you're so sure, Joe?"

"Don't you read the papers, Charlie? The Gallup Poll says Dewey's gonna win 49 to 44 percent. Nobody wants Truman. His own party tried to get General Ike on the ticket instead. Truman can't win, Charlie. He used to work in a clothing store, for goodness sake. What kind of President is that? Let's face it, Charlie, Dewey's in."

Indeed, Joe had some cause for smugness. The Chicago *Daily Tribune* certainly agreed with him. The paper's early edition on the morning after the election ran this big, bold banner headline: DEWEY DEFEATS TRUMAN. Trouble was, the broadly smiling man who held the newspaper high that morning was not Dewey. Instead, blunt, plain-talking Harry S Truman had just pulled off the biggest presidential election upset in U.S. history! He beat Dewey by about two million popular votes and 303 electoral votes to 189. The man who said "the buck stops here"—meaning the person who sits in the Oval Office takes the final responsibility—was back in the White House.

Just how did this earnest, honest, but relatively little-known former senator, given to bursts of temper and salty language, pull off such a political feat? The road to victory began back in Lamar, Missouri, where Harry S Truman was born on May 8, 1884. "S" (without the period) was his real and full middle name. His parents, John Anderson and Martha Ellen Young Truman, didn't want to offend either of his grandfathers, Shippe or Solomon, so they just named him S—no period.

Young Harry, the oldest of three, grew up on farms until the family settled in Independence, Missouri, which Truman later called his hometown. His father was a farmer and livestock salesman who was known as Peanuts because he was very short. Harry grew to about five foot ten inches tall. The elder Truman educated himself and liked to read Shakespeare. Harry's mother was born in Kansas and she never got over the Yankee march into her home state during the Civil War. When her son was President and she spent nights at the White House, she refused to sleep in the Lincoln bed. A college graduate herself, she taught her son to read and followed his career closely until she died at the age of 94, when her oldest child was in the White House.

Truman was a hard-working student who loved to read history, which he continued to do all his life. He wanted to go to West Point or Annapolis, but, unfortunately, he was very near-sighted and had to wear glasses from a very early age. The glasses were expensive so his mother wouldn't let him play sports for fear he would break the specs. Truman later recalled that he was forever running from a fight, and especially when the boys teased him about taking piano lessons.

Harry Truman graduated from Independence High School in 1901. Since the military academies were out because of his poor eyesight and his family couldn't afford college, Truman worked at various jobs—timekeeper, bank teller, mailroom clerk. When the United States entered World War I, his Missouri National Guard unit was called into service. Truman rose from lieutenant to captain and saw action in France. After the war, he and his army buddy, Eddie Jacobson, opened a men's clothing shop. But bad economic times sent it under in 1922 and Truman spent the next 12 years repaying his creditors.

In the meantime, at age 35, Truman had married his childhood sweetheart, Elizabeth "Bess" Wallace of Independence. She was a far better athlete than he, and Harry said he had been in love since the age of six. The two remained devoted through a long marriage, even though Bess hated living in the spotlight of the White House. She died in 1982 at the age of 97, the longest living First Lady ever.

President Truman poses for this picture with his wife, Bess Wallace Truman, and daughter, Margaret, in the Blue Room of the White House.

The Trumans had one daughter, Margaret, who studied history in college and made her singing debut with the Detroit Symphony orchestra in 1947. Today, Margaret Truman Daniels is a well-known writer of mystery novels that use the Washington political scene as background.

But back in 1923, Truman was still without a future, so he enrolled at Kansas City Law School for two years. He was also elected a district judge, which meant that he was the chief executive of Jackson County, Missouri. He did so well at cutting waste and reducing the county debt that he became the county's Democratic leader in 1929. In 1933, President Roosevelt named him re-employment director for the Federal Emergency Relief Administration in Missouri—at the salary of $1 a year!

A year later, Truman was elected to the U.S. Senate, where he gained a reputation as honest and hardworking. He was a loyal supporter of the New Deal and even backed Roosevelt through the "court packing" ruckus. Truman drew some national attention during World War II by exposing waste in military operations. Never one to back off from a good political fight, he loved the rough and tumble of politics. As he was fond of saying, "If you can't stand the heat, stay out of the kitchen." Some government leaders later said they were afraid that Truman's temper might set off World War III.

When Franklin Roosevelt ran for an unheard-of fourth term in 1944, lots of party leaders wanted Vice President Henry Wallace dropped from the ticket because he was too "pro-Russian." A few substitutes were suggested, Truman among them. When Roosevelt called the Democratic National Chairman, Robert Hannegan, to ask if Truman had accepted, Hannegan replied no and that Truman was the "contrariest Missouri mule I've ever dealt with." Actually, Truman didn't want the job. He thought it was useless, a sentiment often echoed through the years. Said Roosevelt to Hannegan, "Tell him if he wants to break up the Democratic party in the middle of a war, that's his responsibility," and hung up. Said Truman, "Why the heck didn't he tell me that in the first place?" and accepted.

Truman was vice president for only a few months when, on the afternoon of April 12, 1945, he was called to the White House. He had no idea that FDR had just died. When he entered, Eleanor Roosevelt said to him, "Harry, the President is dead."

Indeed, he was. The nation was still at war. That evening, Harry S Truman took the oath as the thirty-third President of the United States.

Under a portrait of Woodrow Wilson, Harry Truman is sworn in as President by Justice Harlan F. Stone. In attendance were Cabinet members and leading Congressmen. Mrs. Truman is in center behind her husband and Margaret can be seen behind Justice Stone.

He said to reporters the following day, "I don't know whether you fellows ever had a load of hay fall on you, but when they told me what had happened, I felt like the moon, the stars, and all the planets had fallen on me."

The public saw in Truman a man apparently shaken by the spotlight into which he had been thrust. "If you ever pray, boys," he said to White House reporters soon after he was sworn in, "pray for me now." Would the job prove too much for the feisty man from Missouri who didn't want the job in the first place? Not on your life. What the public could not see, but would come to know and to love, was the determination, backbone, and firmness of purpose of their new President. He might appear to be a humble man, just "one of the guys," and indeed that's how he often sounded. But Harry Truman was supremely confident of his own judgment. You make a decision, you live by it was his philosophy. "That's all there was to it," he often said. The buck did indeed stop in the Oval Office, and when the responsibilities and future of the nation fell on his shoulders, Truman acted with boldness and then never looked back.

In May 1945, a month after Truman took office, Germany surrendered and World War II ended in Europe. But the fighting raged on in the Pacific with promises of yet a long war. Truman met with Winston Churchill and Joseph Stalin in Potsdam that July and August to discuss postwar Europe and to call for Japan's unconditional surrender. It did not come. The new President himself had only the month before learned that FDR had authorized the development of an atomic bomb. Immediately, Truman had set up a committee to discuss the military and moral issues over the use of such a devastating weapon.

Vague warnings of an unidentified, fearful weapon were given to the Japanese leaders. There was still no surrender. The time for a decision was at hand. Once again, the buck had stopped. Even though he feared that its use might bring about the end of the world, President Truman ordered the world's first wartime explosion of an atomic bomb. It fell on the Japanese city of Hiroshima on August 6, 1945. The destruction was awesome. Some sources give the number of deaths, either instantly or within a year from radioactivity, at more than 200,000. Unbelievably, Japan still refused to surrender. Three days later, Truman ordered the strike on Nagasaki. The entire world was stunned and not a little frightened by films of the mushroom-like, spreading clouds rising over the Japanese cities and unleashing unbelievable power. On August 14—V-J Day—Japan agreed to surrender.

Since that time, citizens, educators, military leaders, sociologists, religious groups, and pacifists have debated the morality of Truman's decision to use the atomic bomb. Perhaps the only person who did not second-guess it was the President himself. He had studied the facts and based on those facts, he had made a decision. "That's all there was to it."

Why did Truman decide to drop the bomb? From the information given to him, it was apparent that the war in the Pacific would not end unless and until the Allies invaded the islands of Japan. The estimated cost to Allied troops, based on the difficulty of such an invasion and Japanese fanatic resistance, was as high as one million. In addition, the present advance of the Allies toward Japan was slowed by kamikaze pilots.

The kamikaze was a unique military tactic. Japanese kamikaze pilots were dedicated to deliberately crashing their planes into enemy targets, usually ships. Once strapped in, the pilot had no way to get out of the airplane before it crashed with its

Taken shortly after the atomic bomb was dropped on Hiroshima, this photo shows the extent of the damage to the city's Museum of Science and Industry.

explosive charge. Defending against these suicide attacks was nearly impossible. In one single day on Okinawa, kamikaze pilots killed nearly 5,000 U.S. sailors.

To add to the possibility of more and more casualties, Truman was also troubled by mounting tension with the U.S.S.R. The atomic bombs, which the United States dropped just a few days before the Soviets planned to enter the Pacific fighting, were also intended as a message to the Communists. Soviet aid in the Pacific was no longer necessary.

With the war over, the Soviet Union's obvious intention to install Communist governments in lands occupied by its armies caused Winston Churchill to say that "an iron curtain" was descending over Europe. In what came to be called the Cold War, the United States and the U.S.S.R. were on the brink of nuclear tragedy. In March of 1947, Truman called for the doctrine that bears his name based on the belief that U.S. policy must support

free people everywhere. U.S. military and political support of noncommunist nations was aimed at containing Soviet expansion. He got congressional approval to aid Greece and Turkey with some $400 million, undertook a massive airlift with Great Britain to supply West Berlin when the Soviets isolated the city, and helped establish the military alliance called NATO—the North Atlantic Treaty Organization—against Soviet aggression.

A great deal of credit for Europe's postwar recovery must be given to the so-called Marshall Plan, the European Recovery Program

The Marshall Plan funds even helped former enemies to rebuild after World War II. Here West Berlin workers rebuild Titania Palace, the U.S. sector's largest concert hall and cultural center.

instituted by Secretary of State General George C. Marshall and approved by Truman. It was designed to rehabilitate European nations and create economic conditions that could allow democratic governments to survive. The United States spent some $13 billion between 1948 and 1952 to rebuild Europe from the ashes. The program was highly successful and contributed to the rapid recovery of many countries.

Truman also led the United States in helping to create FDR's dream—the United Nations. It met for the first time in London in 1946 before finding a permanent home in New York City. Through the UN, Truman promoted the creation of the state of Israel in 1948.

As though Europe weren't enough of a problem, Truman had his hands full at home. America was turning its wartime economy back to peace. Such things as gas rationing and food stamps and controls that kept prices down had to be gradually phased out as the nation returned to peacetime living. Rationing of gas and certain food and clothing items was lifted by December 1945, but sugar remained in short supply and was rationed until June 1947. The President especially wanted to hold the line on prices, but Congress disagreed. As a result, price controls were dropped, prices soared, workers wanted higher wages to pay for the more expensive goods. Strikes and the threat of strikes were everywhere. The most serious of such actions came from the United Mine Workers and railroad unions. Truman seized the coal mines and said that he would draft the railroad strikers into the army and send them back to work anyway. The strikes ended.

By the time the 1948 elections rolled around and Truman decided to run, practically everyone was against him. Legislators in Washington were against him, especially as Harry had dubbed them the "do-nothing Eightieth Congress." Certainly railroad workers and coal miners weren't happy with him. The South was against him because of his strong—and unexpected —stand on civil rights issues.

Although the civil rights movement is generally thought of as a phenomenon of the 1950s, when the federal government first took an active part, an important phase of its beginnings can be traced to the realities of World War II. In the military, black Americans had fought for a share of the American dream, only to return home to failure. They had fought for freedom for Europeans, but returned home to the "whites only" signs. African American men and women on the homefront had been hired in record numbers to work in wartime factories. When the soldiers came back, these people once again found that the jobs were for "whites only." A similar situation occurred with women workers of any race. President Truman stood firmly with those who began calling for civil rights changes. This so angered conservative Southern Democrats, or Dixiecrats as they were called, that they even put up their own presidential candidate. Left-wing Democrats organized a third party led by Henry Wallace. Regular Democrats, what was left of the party, were gloomy and shocked. It hadn't occurred to them that Truman would actually try to win an election on his own. They had counted on him just finishing out FDR's term. They had no choice but to accept him. They, too, looked to November and defeat.

Who was there left to vote for feisty Harry and his running mate, Senator Alben Barkley of Kentucky? As it turned out, about 24 million Americans, or enough to put Harry S Truman right back where the buck stops.

How did this miracle upset occur? Perhaps because he was the only one who figured he could win. Whatever the reason, the President set out on a 30,000-mile whistle-stop campaign talking to anyone who would listen. While his Republican opponent, Thomas E. Dewey of New York, was confidently and vaguely talking of national unity and an end to government inefficiency, spunky Harry was waving his fists in the air, and "talking plain." He pledged higher farm price supports, he promised to desegregate the armed forces, he called for a national health insurance program. He told people that if they stayed at home and didn't vote, they'd deserve everything they got.

Then, Harry Truman went home to the White House to wait while all the pollsters predicted his landslide defeat. The rest is history—with an added bonus. Truman even managed to bring in a Democratic Congress once again. So much for the pollsters.

In Truman's State of the Union speech, he proposed the Fair Deal, a 24-plank domestic program. It called for low-cost public housing, expanded Social Security, a fair employment act to prevent discrimination in hiring, and new wage and work laws, among other proposals. But the Eighty-first Congress was in a conservative mood, so many of Truman's ideas were never enacted. However, Congress did pass the Employment Act of 1946, stating government's responsibility for maintaining full employment, raised the minimum wage from 40 cents to 75 cents, extended Social Security benefits to an additional 10 million workers, and promoted slum clearance.

President Truman laughs as he holds an early edition of the Chicago Daily Tribune *announcing his loss of the presidency to Thomas Dewey. The newspaper's erroneous conclusion was based on early election returns.*

Truman's attempt to bring about fair civil rights practices in the United States is often overlooked. Besides desegregating the U.S. armed forces, he called for federal protection of voting rights, for an antilynching law, for a federal agency to regulate equal employment opportunities, and much more. Many of the civil rights laws enacted in the 1960s began with the ideas of the fair-minded thirty-third President of the United States.

The man from Missouri had returned to the White House for a second term—but not for long. In 1949, he noticed that the chandeliers in the grand old mansion were swaying in a rather strange manner. Construction engineers discovered that the White House was "standing up purely by habit." Years of patch-work repairs had finally caught up with the grand old building. It had to be completely overhauled or—unthinkable!—torn down. Congress voted more than $5 million to save the walls, roof, and third floor and gut the entire interior. The Trumans moved across the street to Blair House and did not return until 1952, when the beautifully restored White House was complet-ed, looking just about as it does today.

Meanwhile the nation was entering one of its most shameful periods. With communism on the march around the world, Americans were running scared. Suddenly, it seemed that there was a traitor in every closet. "Communists" were imagined to be cropping up everywhere. In 1946, Truman had okayed a commis-sion to remove people thought to be security risks from sensitive government jobs. The Republican Congress said it didn't go far enough. In 1948, the House Committee on Un-American Activities (HUAC) imprisoned 10 Hollywood screen writers for contempt of Congress. Charged with being Communists, the writers refused to testify against themselves, according to their right under the U.S. Constitution's Fifth Amendment. With the exception of Edward Dmytryk, who admitted "guilt" while in prison, the writers were "blacklisted," never to work in Hollywood again—at least under their own names. None of these people was proved to be a Communist, and in any case, it is not against the law to be a Communist in the United States.

The Red Scare gathered momentum. In 1950, suspected spy Alger Hiss was convicted of giving false testimony to a jury. The following year scientist Julius Rosenberg and his wife, Ethel, were convicted of passing atomic secrets to the Soviets. Hiss served three years of a five-year sentence and was released in

1954, still claiming his innocence. The Rosenbergs were executed in Sing Sing Prison, Ossining, New York, in 1953. They were the first U.S. civilians to be put to death for espionage.

This fear of the Communist menace marched on into the absurd hysteria produced by Senator Joseph McCarthy of Wisconsin. Preying on national fears, he rose to headline prominence on totally groundless claims of knowing over 200 government workers who were Communists. He later downgraded the number to 81 and then 57. McCarthy even charged the Roosevelt and Truman administrations with "treason." Yet, he produced not one shred of evidence to back up his ludicrous charges. He never found one Communist in government, and not one person was even indicted for such. Yet, scores of people lost their jobs and certainly their reputations.

The hysteria reached its low point with the passage of the McCarran Act of 1950. It said all Communists must register with the Justice Department. Now, there was a smart plan! President Truman said it was a bit like asking all cattle rustlers to report to the sheriff. That part of the McCarran Act was declared unconstitutional a few years later.

With the aid of a huge map of the United States, Senator Joseph McCarthy testifies on Communist party organization during the 30-days-long McCarthy-Army hearing in June 1954.

Joseph McCarthy seemed like a man out of control. In 1951, he charged General George C. Marshall, World War II hero and creator of the Marshall Plan, with being a "Communist-dominated traitor." Truman called Marshall "the greatest living American." Marshall won the Nobel Peace Prize in 1953. Joseph McCarthy was finally halted in his Communist witch hunt in 1954, mainly because of his investigation of possible subversion in the United States Army! In a rare move, the U.S. Senate censured him for unbecoming conduct. The censure ended the persecution of innocent persons on the charge of being Communists, known as McCarthyism.

The Red Scare and the Cold War weren't the only problems Truman faced during this period. Unfortunately, the United States was at war again, this time in Korea and this time under the UN banner. At the end of World War II, negotiations had failed to unite Communist North Korea with pro-Western South Korea. The problem was turned over to the United Nations, which called for general elections in the two countries to decide on unification. But the Soviet Union refused to cooperate and a permanent Communist state was established in North Korea. The 38th parallel became the dividing boundary between the two countries. In June 1950, the North Koreans, in a move apparently sanctioned by the Soviets, crossed the 38th parallel and attacked South Korea.

With UN backing, a force led by General Douglas MacArthur, World War II war hero in the Pacific, launched a counteroffensive. He pushed the North Koreans back across the 38th parallel. But China intervened and drove the UN troops, which were actually nearly all American and South Korean, south of the parallel again. MacArthur called for war against China. Truman refused for fear of nuclear war with the Soviets and possibly starting World War III. MacArthur openly criticized U.S. policy. When he did so a second time, the President could tolerate the insubordination no longer. He dismissed the immensely popular war hero and called him home, putting General Matthew Ridgway in his place.

Truman meets with General Douglas MacArthur in October 1950, at Wake Island in the Pacific, shortly before relieving the general of his command in Korea.

Nearly everyone—especially the Republicans—screamed! How could the President treat a larger-than-life war hero in such a manner? Much later, someone suggested that his dismissal of MacArthur was a courageous act. Truman snapped, "Courage didn't have anything to do with it. General MacArthur was insubordinate. I fired him. That's all there was to it."

Peace talks about the Korean War began in 1951, but the fighting dragged on until July 1953, ending with Korea divided, as it remains today. Truman was out of office before the war ended. Although the Twenty-Second Amendment, ratified in 1951, limited all future Presidents to two terms, Truman would have been eligible to run again. He decided not to.

After campaigning for Democrat Adlai Stevenson, who lost to General Dwight D. Eisenhower, in the 1952 election, Harry and Bess went home to Missouri. The media and the public missed the plain-spoken, tell-it-like-it-is President and he was often photographed and quoted on his morning walks around Independence. He died in Kansas City, Missouri, on December 16, 1972, after being in ill health for several years. He is buried in the courtyard of the Truman Library in Independence.

Americans loved Harry Truman because he was honest and frank and incorruptible. Historians generally rank him high on the list of effective chief executives. Britain's Winston Churchill paid him the highest of compliments in the President's last year in office. Said Churchill, "The last time I sat across a conference table from you was at Potsdam. I must confess, sir, I held you in very low regard. I misjudged you badly. Since that time, you more than any other man saved Western civilization."

Well, the great Churchill wasn't the only one to misjudge Harry S Truman. Political pollsters had botched it up, too. During his years in office, he was generally looked upon as being too small for the task at hand. It is true that Truman may not have been prepared to lead the country when fate put him in the White House. But he became that rare individual, a person who grows into the job. It was only after he left office that his true leadership abilities were recognized to their fullest. Those who lived through the Truman era still hold him in very high—and affectionate—regard. When the nation needed a strong, decisive, no-nonsense leader, Harry Truman did his darndest. As the thirty-third President himself might have said, "That's all there was to it."

Names in the News in Truman's Time

Thomas E. Dewey (1902–1971):

Born Michigan; New York governor (1942–1954); surprised nearly everyone by losing to Truman in 1948 presidential election.

Enrico Fermi (1901–1954):

Italian-born physicist; produced first self-sustaining nuclear chain reaction in history at University of Chicago (1942). Coded telegram to Washington announcing the feat said: "The Italian navigator has entered the new world."

John L. Lewis (1880–1969):

Bushy-eyebrowed labor leader; head of United Mine Workers, who tormented FDR and Truman throughout WWII with defiance and strikes in an effort to strengthen workers' union.

Joe DiMaggio (1914–):

"Joltin' Joe," all-time baseball great, known as the "Yankee Clipper." N.Y. Yankees outfielder (1936–1951); batted safely in record 56 consecutive games. Hall of Famer (1955).

Ethel and Julius Rosenberg (1915/1918–1951):

Both born New York City; first U.S. civilians put to death for espionage. Convicted of giving U.S. nuclear secrets to the Soviets; executed Sing Sing prison, Ossining, NY.

When United Mine Workers leader, John L. Lewis, threatened a coal strike during World War II, Congress faced off with an antistrike bill that allowed the President to seize closed factories and to require "cooling-off" periods prior to any walkouts.

Dwight D. Eisenhower (1953-1961)

"*I* like Ike!" "I like Ike!" declared the campaign buttons in 1952. And why not? Dwight David Eisenhower was a genuine war hero. During World War II in 1942, he became commanding general of U.S. forces in Europe. He was in charge of the greatest invasion force ever assembled, the Allied landings in France on June 6, 1944—D-Day. Its success, brought about in part by Eisenhower's gamble on the weather, signaled the beginning of the end of Axis control in Europe. A military man for most of his adult life, Eisenhower attained that rare lofty perch—a five-star general.

All during the war, Americans had gotten used to seeing the broad grin on the general who displayed a good deal of fruit salad on the jacket of his army pinks. The U.S. Army dress uniform was referred to as "pinks" for the unusual shade of the light-colored trousers. "Fruit salad" is the nonmilitary designation for the ribbon bars of various colors and patterns worn on the left side of a uniform of any service branch. They designate medals won or places or wars in which the person has served. Ike came home a hero and changed the pinks for a gray-flannel suit. However, it may well have been the conflict in Korea, not his exploits in World War II, that put him in the White House as the thirty-fourth President of the United States.

His real name was David Dwight, the third of seven sons born to David Jacob and Ida Stover Eisenhower. One child died in infancy. To avoid confusion with his father, the future general

46

was called by his middle name, which he began using exclusively after he entered West Point. At one time or another, all of the six Eisenhower boys were known as "Ike"!

The third Ike was born near Denison, Texas, on October 14, 1890. A year later, the family moved to Abilene, Kansas, where he grew up. His father was a mechanic and the family was poor. All the boys were expected to help out. Early on, Ike learned the value of hard work. He also learned what he later called the most valuable lesson of his life. As a youngster, he once got so angry at being disciplined that he beat his knuckles bloody against a tree. As his mother nursed his wounds, she talked about the uselessness of hatred. Ike never forgot the lesson. For all his adult life, he tried to avoid criticizing anyone and kept a generally sunny disposition. When he was 15, he scraped his leg and developed blood poisoning. The doctors recommended amputation to save his life. Ike told his brother Edgar to stand guard at the door. No one was going to cut off his leg! The doctor kept warning about the possibility of death, but young Eisenhower persisted. The leg healed and Ike had learned another important lesson, the importance of willpower. Eisenhower was interested in sports at Abilene High School, but was a mediocre student. After his graduation in 1909, he worked for a year to help support the college education of one of his brothers. Attracted by the promise of a free education, he then applied to both the U.S. Naval Academy at Annapolis and the U.S. Military Academy at West Point. He passed the naval exam, but, at age 20, was past the age to enter Annapolis. Ike became a West Point cadet in 1911. Still an average student, he was a fine football player until he injured his knee.

Eisenhower graduated 61st of 164 cadets, with engineering as his best subject. He earned several demerits, however, for being late to class or drills. His West Point graduating class of 1915, about to enter a period that would include two world wars, would produce 59 generals!

Dwight and Mamie Eisenhower posed for this photo three days after their wedding on July 1, 1916. At the time Eisenhower was stationed at Fort Sam Houston near San Antonio, Texas.

The brand new second lieutenant was sent to Fort Sam Houston in San Antonio, Texas, where romance entered his life. Pretty Mamie Doud was the daughter of a well-to-do meat packer from Denver. Mamie and Ike were married in 1916. Their first child died of scarlet fever at the age of four. Their second son, John, was born in 1922. John Doud Eisenhower would also graduate from West Point and become a general. John's own son, David, Ike's grandson, would later marry Julie Nixon, the younger daughter of President Richard M. Nixon.

Although Eisenhower was promoted to captain and commanded a tank training center during World War I, he was not sent overseas. In the years leading to World War II, his military career jumped on the fast track. He served in the Panama Canal Zone and, in 1926, graduated first in his class from the Command General Staff School at Fort Leavenworth, Kansas. From there it was the Army War College, duty in France, and, in 1933, on to General Douglas MacArthur's staff in Washington, D.C. Ike was one of the young military officers ordered by President Herbert Hoover to clear out the Bonus Marchers, veterans during the Depression who were demanding their pensions. After serving as MacArthur's aide in the Philippines, Eisenhower came back to the United States, where he was promoted to full colonel in 1941 and was named chief of staff of the U.S. Third Army.

By late 1941, Eisenhower was a brigadier general and by March of the following year, he was promoted to major general and named head of the operations division of the War Department. That June, General George C. Marshall, army chief of staff, selected Ike over 366 senior officers to command all U.S. troops in Europe.

Why? Was Dwight Eisenhower such a brilliant or great general that he deserved the promotion over more senior men? The answer is no. Ike was a rather modest man, friendly and likeable, not dashing and forceful like MacArthur, for instance, or full of color and bravado like George Patton. If he showed brilliance at all, it was in military strategy, organization, and administration. Ike was a good general, not a great one. So why was he picked to lead U.S. troops and why did President Roosevelt name him Supreme Commander of the Allied Expeditionary Forces to lead the D-Day invasion of France? Mainly because Ike had what the others did not, the ability to persuade and to mediate, to hold together differing personalities and forces and blend them into one cohesive fighting unit. That is not a quality to be taken lightly especially in wartime. Perhaps no other person could have done it so well.

Ike's—and the Allied forces'—crowning military achievement was the invasion of France on June 6, 1944. Its code name was Operation Overlord, but it is known as D-Day, which actually means the first day of any military operation. This was the largest invasion fleet ever assembled—hundreds of thousands of troops and about 4,000 ships of all types. They crossed the English Channel to land in

General Eisenhower talks with paratroopers in England just prior to their departure for the first assault in the invasion of Europe at Normandy, France, on June 6, 1944.

Normandy on the northern coast of France. The success of this operation marked the beginning of the end of the war in Europe.

Secrecy for D-Day was critical. The enemy, of course, knew that an invasion was planned—but where or when? The fact that the Allies were able to surprise on both counts is amazing in itself. Timing for the operation was critical, too. Hundreds of thousands of lives and tons of equipment were at stake. So was the war. Favorable weather and tides narrowed the choices to June 5, 6, or 7. Eisenhower chose June 5.

By that day, the worst weather in the English Channel in years had rolled in. The invasion was delayed for 24 hours. As June 6 neared, Eisenhower faced his greatest dilemma. The forecast again called for threatening weather with a possibility of clearing. If he called off the invasion, the tides would not be favorable for another two weeks. The chances of keeping such a huge operation secret for that much longer were slim. But if he gave the go-ahead sign and the weather worsened, the entire invasion, even the war, might be lost. So would thousands and thousands of lives. After weighing the odds, steady and sure Dwight Eisenhower decided the odds were on his side. Operation Overlord was a go.

In the early morning hours of June 6, 1944, under cloudy skies that did eventually clear, the world's largest invasion force began its dangerous crossing. The United States suffered about 10,000 casualties in that operation. But the Allies had landed and they would not be thrown back.

By the end of June, the Allies were fighting toward the heart of France. Paris was liberated on August 25. That December Eisenhower was honored with the highest ranking a U.S. soldier can receive. The President named him a five-star general, a newly created rank, which was also awarded to Henry (Hap) Arnold, Douglas MacArthur, and George Marshall. The last general to receive five stars was Omar Bradley, who was promoted to that rank in 1950.

The Allies crossed the Rhine River into Germany in March 1945. The Germans surrendered on May 7, and World War II was over in Europe.

Ike came home in June 1945 and received a hero's welcome as the most popular and respected soldier in the nation. He retired from the army in early 1948 and became president of Columbia University in New York City. He also published a book, *Crusade in Europe*.

But the army had not prepared the old soldier for the academic life, and he was largely a figurehead at Columbia, out of his element. At President Truman's request, Ike gladly took over command of the North Atlantic Treaty Organization (NATO) and performed well until he returned home from Europe in 1952.

Political leaders had long been after the general to run for the presidency. Ike would have none of it. In fact, in a letter to a newpaper publisher in 1948, Eisenhower commented that spending one's life in the military does not qualify a person for political office. That rather remarkable statement from a lifetime military man, of course, only endeared him all the more to the public.

It was a little difficult at first to get Eisenhower on a presidential ticket because no one knew whether he was a Republican or Democrat. Finally, he decided he was a Republican and agreed to run in the 1952 election, with Richard M. Nixon of California as his running mate.

Ike the war hero faced Democrat Adlai A. Stevenson of Illinois, a witty and intellectual opponent. Eisenhower was a poor campaigner, friendly but vague and somewhat aloof. Yet, it may have been what he said and wrote about the ongoing war in Korea that put him in the White House. He felt that the horror of World War II should add up to more than just honoring the dead. At least, the deaths and suffering and devastation should result in a better world. But he worried that the conflict in Korea might mean that the Cold War turned to hot, the beginning of World War III.

In August, during the 1952 election campaign, Eisenhower hosts Republican party national committee women from eleven states at his Commodore Hotel headquarters in New York City.

Americans worried, too. And when Ike promised "I shall go to Korea" if elected and try to bring peace, he clinched the victory.

For the first time in a presidential election, television became a factor. This was a time when intellectuals, such as Stevenson, were called "eggheads." It was not meant to be flattering. Eisenhower appeared on the TV screen as friendly and reassuring. He flashed the familiar grin in a grandfatherly way, and America responded. "I like Ike" was the slogan on everybody's lips.

Eisenhower entered the White House carrying all but nine states and gaining more than six million votes over Stevenson. Ike even brought the Republicans into control of Congress on his political coattails, but that lasted only two years.

Although Eisenhower held no strong political views on either side, he did employ mostly conservative advisers and so was thought of as basically conservative himself. He ran the government a good deal like he ran the military. He delegated authority. In fact, he was criticized for giving too much authority to his assistant, the former New Hampshire governor, Sherman Adams, who became the President's most influential adviser. Adams resigned in September 1958 over accepting an illegal gift. Ike was also criticized for not criticizing Senator Joseph McCarthy and his anticommunist hysteria. Although Ike privately detested the senator, he refused to condemn McCarthy publicly in order to preserve party unity. Eisenhower was forever the mediator.

The old general did go to Korea as he had promised to take a personal hand in peace negotiations. Ike did not bring about peace; the North Koreans and their Chinese allies had already decided to stop fighting. But Ike did resist the urging of the South Koreans to move into North Korean territory. The peace treaty was signed in July 1953. About 34,000 Americans died in the war, which left North and South Korea split as before at the 38th parallel. The Korean War did prove two things. In the nuclear age, a war could be fought without nuclear weapons, and the United Nations could be counted on to fight aggression. More than half a century later, the first assumption still holds, but the second has been severely tested in many parts of the world.

For a country yearning for peace after war and for a President who exuded calm and serenity, the Eisenhower years were marked by some extraordinary—and threatening—incidents, both domestic and abroad.

In 1954, Eisenhower had been instrumental, along with his secretary of state, John Foster Dulles, in creating the Southeast Asia Treaty Organization (SEATO) to prevent the spread of communism in that part of the world. In 1956, Egypt announced that it was taking over the Suez Canal in the Mediterranean from British authority. After negotiations failed, a force of British, French, and Israeli troops retook the canal. But they pulled out when Eisenhower and the United Nations condemned their action, leaving the canal under Egypt's control. With the Soviet Union backing Egypt, Eisenhower feared a Communist takeover in that strategic region. He urged Congress to adopt what came to be known as the Eisenhower Doctrine (1957), a pledge that the United States would go to the aid of any Middle Eastern country that asked for help against Communist aggression. That July,

Lebanon called for aid against a Communist armed rebellion. Ike sent in some 1,400 soldiers and marines, and the crisis passed. Another crisis appeared in the summer of 1958 when the Communist Chinese bombed the islands of Quemoy and Matsu, where Nationalist Chinese troops had been building up forces. Ike waited quietly until the Communists lost interest and stopped the bombing.

According to the old proverb, "time and tide wait for no man"; neither do U.S. presidential elections. Crisis or no, the 1956 campaign was at hand, with the opposition, as before, "egghead" Adlai Stevenson. Against the overwhelmingly popular President, the Democrats did have one critical issue—but they couldn't even talk about it, at least directly. It was not domestic or foreign policy, but the President's health. In September 1955, Ike had a heart attack. An anxious public was issued almost hourly reports until Americans were reassured by the sight of him on the hospital balcony a month later wearing bright red pajamas that said, "Much Better, Thanks." This was followed in June 1956, by an emergency operation for an intestinal problem. Constant and endless reports of this condition followed as well. Before the Democrats could even hint that he wasn't up to another term, his doctors said he was, and Ike set off on a fairly active campaign swing. The public loved him even more. Of course, the Suez crisis helped a little. It said, "See, experience counts in the White House!" This time, Ike beat Stevenson by more than nine and a half million votes, the most lopsided win

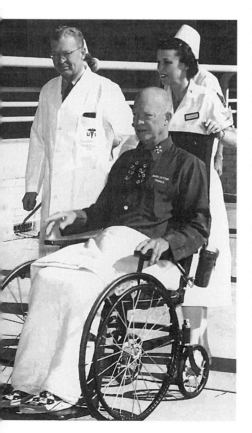

Sporting his Supreme Commander's five gold stars plus a silver one for "good conduct" from his doctor, Eisenhower recovers from his 1955 heart attack at Fitzsimons Army Medical Center in Aurora, Colorado.

since Roosevelt in 1936. The electoral vote count was 457 to 73. Eisenhower was able to finish his second term, even though he did suffer a slight stroke in 1957.

Probably the most serious challenge to Eisenhower's presidency occurred in late 1957. Three years earlier, in a landmark decision (*Brown v. the Board of Education of Topeka*, 1954), the U.S. Supreme Court had struck down a long-held practice. Said the Court, separate is not equal. Racial segregation in U.S. public schools was declared unconstitutional. The nation seemed stunned at first. Then, gaining momentum, students and other protesters began to march and picket for civil rights. The protests often turned violent, especially in some parts of the South. In September 1957, Arkansas Governor Orval E. Faubus declared he would obstruct a federal court order to integrate Little Rock's all-white Central High School.

What would President Eisenhower do? Although he had always declared himself against racial segregation, he had been criticized by civil rights advocates for failing to take a strong stand. This time he did. On September 25, 1957, Eisenhower sent 1,000 federal troops to Little Rock. The nation was silenced by the sight of U.S. soldiers protecting nine frightened African American children as they walked slowly into Little Rock Central High. America's most painful domestic problem, the issue of discrimination and civil rights, had been largely hidden since the country's birth. It began to come to the surface after World War II and now, in the 1950s, it was bursting wide open.

The weak Civil Rights Act of 1957, which protected voting rights, was the first such national law passed since 1875. Other far-reaching and more radical legislation would follow in the 1960s. The country would reach a new militancy as black Americans and their white supporters grew dissatisfied with the slow progress of nonviolent protest. Although the fight to end discrimination went on, it had become less militant by the 1990s. Civil rights advocates now seek political office and other legislative means to end still painful abuses.

Ten days after the Little Rock episode, Americans were hit with another blow to national pride. This one knocked the "We-won-the-war-and-we-are-the-best" feeling right into the next century. On October 4, 1957, the Soviet Union launched *Sputnik I*, the first manufactured satellite to orbit the Earth. Suddenly, the United States was only second best at something. It was an unfamiliar and uneasy feeling. At first fearful of being spied on by the Russians and then angry because we weren't first, Americans—for the first time—began to cast some blame on the popular President. Many said it proved what they had long thought, that Eisenhower was just letting the government drift along in an easygoing way, not leading or pushing it anywhere. The Eisenhower administration had advocated low military budgets and had not developed a space program. However, the United States launched its first satellite, *Explorer I*, in January 1958, and with Eisenhower's support, the National Aeronautics and Space Administration (NASA) was created that July. However, the Soviet Union would lead the space race until the successful U.S. landing on the moon in 1969.

Although the President remained ever popular with the people, his administration began to draw more and more criticism, especially in foreign policy. It was accused of being "all talk," and there were several instances to back up the complaints. Both Secretary Dulles and Eisenhower spoke of liberating all peoples of Eastern Europe. Yet, when uprisings broke out in East Germany in 1953 and in Hungary in 1956, where the Soviets crushed a revolt for independence, the United States did little more than protest. In 1954, Eisenhower refused when France called for U.S. aid against the uprising in its Southeast Asian colony of Vietnam. The Vietnamese threw out the French, and the countries of North Vietnam, controlled by the Communists, and South Vietnam were established. Eisenhower did show concern that communism would take over that entire area, however, when he talked about setting up a row of dominoes and knocking over just one. This came to be known as the "domino theory," meaning that if one small nation in an area goes Communist, one by one the others will, too. It dominated American foreign policy and kept the U.S. government focused on a strategy of containment, meaning confining Communist takeovers to a limited area. All too soon, Americans would learn that the unrest in Vietnam was only the beginning of a long and indecisive conflict.

Before he left office, Eisenhower tried for a last conference to ease Cold War tensions between the Soviet Union and the United States. It was set for May 16, 1960, in Paris. On May 1, a U-2 reconnaissance spy plane was shot down over Russia. It turned out to be American, and the pilot was Francis Gary Powers, who was captured. After some faint denials, the President had to admit that he was responsible for the spy mission, although he expressed no regrets. The summit collapsed. Powers was convicted of spying but exchanged for a Soviet spy in 1962. Soviet-American relations were, to say the least, strained when the new President, John F. Kennedy, took over in 1961.

Kennedy would also become involved in the last crisis of the Eisenhower administration. Just weeks before Ike left office, the United States broke off relations with Fidel Castro, Communist dictator who now controlled the island of Cuba, 90 miles off the Florida coast.

Ike and Mamie Eisenhower went home to their farm in Gettysburg, Pennsylvania, having left the country larger than before. Both Alaska and

While President and afterward, Eisenhower enjoyed an occasional game of golf. Here he plays before a crowd of spectators at a course near Ottawa, Canada, in July 1958.

Hawaii had been admitted as the forty-ninth and fiftieth states, respectively, in 1959. Ike played golf a lot and wrote his memoirs. After suffering several heart attacks, he died on March 18, 1969, and is buried in Abilene, Kansas, as is Mamie, who died in 1979. Her birthplace in Boone, Iowa, is a historic site. Mamie Eisenhower and Abigail Adams are the only two First Ladies to be so honored.

The Eisenhower years? So much crisis and turmoil for an administration that showed such promise of calm and serenity. In truth, of course, the events would have occurred, to one degree or other, no matter who lived in the White House. The times, they truly "were a'changin'." It can be said with some truth that over any eight-year period, from one two-term President to the next, many, many changes will have occurred. Perhaps that was never more true than during the Eisenhower years when the changes that had been brewing after World War II erupted into full-blown discontent. After a long and devastating war, the American people yearned for comfort and the good old days. But the people and the country were different, and the good old days were gone. Soldiers—black and white—came back to a nation that had changed considerably. In increasing numbers, women would no longer be content to be homemakers alone. Many of them had been out in the working world, and they were not going back. African Americans had fought for a better world right along with their white counterparts; they were not going back either.

The Eisenhower years have been criticized for drift and complacency, and perhaps rightly so. Ike did not change the office or put a personal stamp upon it as some have done before and since. He was the first military leader to become President since Ulysses S. Grant, 84 years earlier. Yet, Ike seemed more a comforting grandfather than a stern general, and wasn't that perhaps just what the country wanted and needed? There would be time for protest marches and Vietnam and corruption in government and assassinations and all sorts of turmoil to test the American courage and character. But when Eisenhower came home, the people had just returned to peace and they still felt as though they needed a simple place. The slogan said "I like Ike." For a few short years, that was comfort enough.

Names in the News in Eisenhower's Time

John Foster Dulles (1888–1959):

Ike's secretary of state (1953–1959); given unprecedented authority in shaping American foreign policy.

William Faulkner (1897–1962):

Mississippi-born, leading U.S. novelist; winner of Nobel prize (1949) and Pulitzer prizes (1954, 1963). Best known for *The Sound and the Fury* (1929), *Absalom! Absalom!* (1936), *A Fable* (1954), *The Reivers* (1962).

Ernest Hemingway (1899–1961):

Noted U.S. novelist and short story writer; born in Illinois. Pulitzer prize (1952); Nobel prize (1954). Best known for *A Farewell to Arms* (1929), *For Whom the Bell Tolls* (1940), *The Old Man and the Sea* (1953).

J. Edgar Hoover (1895–1972):

FBI director (1926–1972), freed the department from political control; criticized in later years for authoritarianism.

Grace Kelly (1929–1982):

Philadelphia-born actress whose beauty and talent won her national acclaim; best actress Oscar for *The Country Girl* (1954); retired to marry Prince Rainier of Monaco (1956).

Robert A. Taft (1889–1953):

Known as Mr. Republican, son of 27th U.S. President. Lost 1952 presidential nomination to Eisenhower, spent following year supporting the President's programs.

J. Edgar Hoover was often the target of the cartoonist. Here he is caricatured by Al Hirshfeld in 1971.

Chapter Four

Kennedy and the Myth of Camelot

John F. Kennedy (1961-1963)

*I*n a splendid time long ago, King Arthur and his Knights of the Round Table held court in the mythical land of Camelot. This wondrous, magical place formed the background of a smash Broadway musical of the same name. The celebrated team of Alan Lerner, with his clever words, and Frederick Lowe, with his beautiful music, enraptured audiences with a tale of a land so congenial that rain fell only after sundown and July was never too hot. In short, all who lived in Camelot lived happily ever after.

After President John Kennedy was assassinated in 1963, his youthful admirers began to speak of his 1,037 days in office as a shining Camelot. They spoke not of what his administration had accomplished, but what it had promised.

Camelot is a myth, make believe. And in some ways, ironically, so were the Kennedy days. The President was youthful looking and handsome, with reddish brown hair and blue eyes. Tall and well built, he was the very picture of glowing health. In fact, he was anything but healthy. As a child, he suffered from a weak and often painful back, and the condition was aggravated by injury in World War II. Operations on his back nearly killed him, and he was never without pain and a back brace during the days of his presidency. His left leg was shorter than his right and he wore corrective shoes. He also suffered from Addison's disease, a blood disorder that interferes with the function of the adrenal glands. These glands, one on the upper end of each kidney, regulate the flow of sodium and potassium in the blood. The disease can be controlled, as in Kennedy's case, by medicine.

Jack and the beautiful, elegant First Lady, Jacqueline, were the nation's most admired couple. Well dressed, wealthy, sophisticated, and charming, theirs was the very model of the perfect marriage. But after his death, Kennedy's involvements with other women were publicized.

On Inauguration Day in 1961, President John F. Kennedy proclaimed that "the torch has been passed to a new generation of Americans." His relative youth, as well as his charisma, was important in his election for, despite his war service, he seemed to represent, for the first time, a generation of Americans who knew neither war nor depression. He promised to use all his vitality to get the country moving again, to put a fire under the sluggish economy, to overtake the Soviet Union in nuclear missiles, to ease unemployment, and to right the wrongs of discrimination.

The American public believed Kennedy's energy and his words. Were they, too, a myth? On that score, the jury stays forever out. Kennedy was assassinated in the third year of his presidency. Who knows if all his promises were real and if his energy could have carried them through. Could the Kennedy years indeed have passed the torch to a new generation of Americans? Or, was it all just Camelot?

John Fitzgerald Kennedy, called Jack by his friends, was born into a somewhat Camelot-like world. His wealthy parents were the aristocrats of the Irish Catholic community in Boston. Jack was the second son of Joseph Patrick and Rose Fitzgerald Kennedy. His father made a fortune in the stock market and was known as a shrewd dealer. His maternal grandfather, John F. "Honey Fitz" Fitzgerald, for whom he was named, was mayor of Boston. His paternal grandfather, Patrick J. Kennedy, was one of the city's most powerful political leaders.

Jack was born in Brookline, Massachusetts, on May 29, 1917, the first President to be born in the twentieth century. By the time the eighth and last of his siblings, Edward (Teddy), was born in 1932, the family home was a rambling summer house in Hyannis Port on Cape Cod.

The Kennedys grew up under the stern—almost ruthless—drive of their father, who instilled in all the children a fierce desire to win—at anything. Jack later said that his father had very high standards for his children and he could be very tough if those standards weren't met. Joe senior also instilled in them an obligation to repay the society from which they benefited so handsomely. Jack was an active but sickly child. His brothers said he was so sick all the time that a mosquito took a risk in biting him!

All during his youth, Jack walked in the shadow of the oldest of the Kennedy kids, Joe junior. Joe was good at everything. Jack, although intelligent and able, managed only a lackluster C grade at exclusive Choate Academy. His friends at Choate called him "rat face" because he was so skinny. He kept up his C average at Princeton University, having decided not to follow Joe to Harvard. However, after two years he did transfer to Harvard University and then took off a semester to accompany his father to Europe. The elder Kennedy had been named by President Roosevelt as ambassador to England.

Jack's travels across Europe as the storm clouds gathered for World War II deeply disturbed and changed him. He returned to Harvard with a new interest in his studies. His thesis, called *Why England Slept*, concerned how the Allies ignored the rise of Hitler. Published as a book, it was a best-seller. By the time he graduated with honors in June 1940, young Kennedy was already a millionaire, having received that sum from his father on his twenty-first birthday.

When the United States entered World War II after Pearl Harbor, Kennedy volunteered for the army. He was turned down because of his back. However, he was able to enlist in the navy as a seaman. His father's influence got him a commission, and as an ensign, he was given command of a small patrol craft known as a PT boat. On the night of August 2, 1943, then-Lieutenant Kennedy's PT-109 was hit by a Japanese destroyer in the South Pacific. Two members of the crew died, and Kennedy, despite his weak back, kept one of the crew afloat for hours until they reached an island where they were rescued days later. For this, Kennedy won a Purple Heart medal.

On June 12, 1944, Kennedy received the Navy and Marine Corps medal for extremely heroic conduct while commanding a PT boat in the Pacific from Captain Frederic L. Conklin.

Jack Kennedy's political career began when he ran for the House of Representatives in 1946. With this first political race began the Kennedy formula for winning. Have the whole clan come and help out! Brother Bobby, age 20 and just home from the navy, became manager. The Kennedy sisters handed out literature and campaigned for Jack.

The Kennedy blitz worked, and Jack entered the House at the age of 29. He was so young looking that some of the members thought he was one of the elevator operators. But by 1952, Kennedy already had his eye on higher stakes—the Senate. As a Democrat, he managed to unseat the respected senator from Massachusetts, Henry Cabot Lodge, even while Eisenhower and the Republicans were sweeping the country.

The society wedding of the year took place on September 12, 1953, when the 36-year-old senator married socialite Jacqueline Bouvier, 24, of Newport, Rhode Island. Jackie, as she came to be known affectionately to the public, was wealthy, beautiful, educated, intelligent, and charming. They became a fairy-tale

Jacqueline Lee Bouvier and Senator John F. Kennedy pose at the door of St. Mary's Roman Catholic Church in Newport, Rhode Island, after their wedding, September 12, 1953.

couple, eventually with two fairy-tale children, elfin Caroline, born in 1957, and playful John junior, known as John John, born 1960, who was often photographed in the Oval Office sitting under his father's desk. A third Kennedy child, named Patrick, died shortly after birth in 1963.

As a senator, Kennedy befriended the working force and was critical of the Eisenhower Cold War policies. But he drew much heat because of his passive attitude toward Senator Joe McCarthy, who was conducting a Communist witch hunt throughout the country. In truth, McCarthy was a personal friend of brother Bobby, and Jack didn't want to speak against him. When the Senate voted to censure McCarthy, Jack was absent. Critics said he was ducking the issue, even though it was expected that he would have voted for censure along with the others. Actually, Kennedy was in the hospital at the time recovering from back surgery, which nearly caused his death.

During a six-month recuperation at his parents' home in Palm Beach, Florida, Kennedy lay strapped to a board. To help pass the time, he wrote a biography of eight American political leaders who had taken unpopular stands. It was called *Profiles in Courage*, and it won him the Pulitzer Prize for biography in 1957.

Friends say that Kennedy decided to run for the presidency while in Florida. But, of course, winning was impossible. How could John Fitzgerald Kennedy become President of the United States? He was Roman Catholic, and the popular wisdom had long stated that no Catholic could win. Many Americans truly believed that a Catholic President would be subject to the dictates of the pope, the head of the Roman Catholic Church in Rome. In fact, the fear of "popery" in Boston dated back to before the U.S. Constitution. It may seem strange to Americans today, but at that time it was a very real concern, and Jack Kennedy's election went a long way to proving that popular wisdom wrong.

In the 1956 election, Kennedy narrowly missed becoming Adlai Stevenson's running mate against Eisenhower. That spot went to Senator Estes Kefauver of Tennessee. The Democrats had no chance against Ike anyway, but Kennedy campaigned tirelessly for the losing ticket. Almost overnight the handsome young senator became a political favorite.

According to Theodore H. White, who wrote a book about the making of the President in 1960, Kennedy's decision to seek the nomination was made at a conference in Hyannis Port in late 1959. Those at the meeting included Jack, his brothers Bobby and Ted, and their father. Said White, they were there to make a President, "with greater precision, against greater odds, across more contrary traditions, than had been shown by any group of amateur President makers since Abraham Lincoln's backers, a century before, had changed the structure of nineteeth-century politics."

And so they did. It was not, however, easy. In the first place, no person had gone from the Senate directly to the White House—with one exception, Warren G. Harding. But with the scandal of the Harding administration, no one wanted to bring that up. In the second place, Kennedy had some formidable rivals waiting for a chance at the top job. They were all senators: Hubert H. Humphrey of Minnesota, Stuart Symington of

Missouri, and Lyndon B. Johnson of Texas, and they all had more experience than Kennedy. In the third place, there was the Catholic issue again.

Kennedy faced the Catholic issue head on. In a televised speech, he declared his belief in the separation of Church and State. Then he went against Humphrey in the economically poor and overwhelmingly Protestant state of West Virginia. If a rich man's son, and a Catholic to boot, could win there, he could certainly win the White House. Charismatic young Kennedy got 61 percent of the vote and knocked Humphrey out of the race.

In September of the 1960 election campaign, Kennedy addresses this large crowd in New Jersey.

Kennedy was nominated on the first ballot at the Democratic convention in Los Angeles in July 1960. He chose rival Lyndon Johnson as his running mate, supposedly to gain southern support since Johnson was from Texas. However, an aide later said that Kennedy also wanted Johnson out of the Senate, where it was feared that he would be against some of Kennedy's programs. When Kennedy accepted the nomination, he said that "We stand today on the edge of the New Frontier—the frontier of the 1960s..." The New Frontier became part of his election campaign and his administration.

The 1960 presidential election race, pitting Democrat John F. Kennedy against Republican Richard M. Nixon, was a wonder of modern advertising techniques and superb strategy. Brother Bobby, Kennedy's campaign manager, was a matchless organizer, and, of course, there was the Kennedy clan helping out at every opportunity. But most of all, there was Jack

Kennedy himself, personable, charismatic, full of hope for the future. In addition, there was his beautiful and charming wife, Jacqueline, and adorable daughter Caroline. John junior was born shortly after Election Day.

Even so, with all that organization, charm, and help, John Kennedy became the thirty-fifth President of the United Sates by the narrowest popular margin in the twentieth century! Out of some 69 million votes cast, only 120,000 votes separated Kennedy and Nixon.

Kennedy was helped somewhat by the votes of many African Americans because he had openly championed the fight for civil rights by black leader Martin Luther King, Jr. But many political observers say it wasn't civil rights or charm or organization or issues that won the election for Kennedy. It was television. The age of visual politics had begun. In a series of four debates, Kennedy and Nixon faced each other and debated questions. Both showed a good grasp of the issues. But television is visual above all, and Kennedy just looked better. He was tanned, healthy appearing, and fit. Nixon looked pale, tired, and uncharacteristically unsure of himself. Experts called the debates a draw on the issues, but that was a plus for Kennedy because he proved that he could handle himself against the more experienced opponent. Kennedy himself later said he doubted he would have won without the television debates.

Kennedy on the left and Richard M. Nixon during their second televised debate. These 1960 debates were the first televised, an occurrence that has taken place during every presidential election since.

Just how crucial a role television played in the election of 1960 is shown in the polls taken just after the Kennedy-Nixon debates. Those who watched them on television gave a good edge to Kennedy. Those who did not see the candidates, but only heard them on radio, gave a slight edge to Nixon.

John F. Kennedy became the first Roman Catholic, and the youngest man, at age 43, ever elected President of the United States. When he took office on January 20, 1961, he was the second youngest man ever to serve, Theodore Roosevelt having become President at the age of 42 on the death of McKinley.

It was a memorable Inauguration Day in many ways in the nation's capital. The air was clear but cold. Side by side, the Presidents made a stirring contrast, both men resplendent in top hats and coattails. The elderly outgoing President, Dwight Eisenhower, was turning over the reins of government to the energetic and young new leader. It seemed to symbolize a change in the country. The complacent, good old days were over; it was time to push up the shirtsleeves and get working. "Let's get America moving again," Kennedy had urged. His inauguration speech was one of the more memorable in history. He implored fellow Americans to "ask not what your country can do for you—ask what you can do for your country."

John F. Kennedy takes the oath of office as President from Supreme Court Justice Earl Warren. Jackie Kennedy is on the far left, and Richard Nixon on the far right.

With new energy, with a vision of a better world for all, and for young people a feeling that this government was not for their elders but for them, the Kennedy era began. It would last just 1,037 days and in its wake would follow some of America's most chaotic domestic crises.

The top hats had hardly come off and the music of the inaugural balls had hardly died down before experts were already praising the next 100 days. They likened Kennedy's probable accomplishments to the FDR administration in 1933. Then came the Bay of Pigs.

On April 17, 1961, the President plunged into his first international crisis. It was a disaster. On that day, some 1,500 Cuban exiles, trained and armed by the U.S. Central Intelligence Agency (CIA), invaded the island of Cuba, off the Florida coast, at Cochinos Bay (Bay of Pigs). Exiled Cubans living in the United States had long wanted to overthrow Fidel Castro, the Communist revolutionary who had taken over Cuba in 1959. Of course, the United States also wanted Castro out.

Eisenhower had okayed the Bay of Pigs mission. Kennedy knew about it and had approved it. The Joint Chiefs of Staff—the top U.S. military advisers—had assured Kennedy of its success. They said that when the exiles landed to start the invasion, the Cuban people would rise up and join them. The exiles landed and were all killed or captured. No one joined them, not even U.S. forces. Kennedy had promised air support, but the planes arrived too soon. Kennedy accepted total blame for the disaster.

International problems continued to plague him. Older world leaders questioned his experience. Soviet leader Nikita Khrushchev decided to test it. During the ongoing Cold War between the two nations, Khrushchev had a wall built between East and West Berlin and threatened to sign a private peace treaty with East Germany. Kennedy called U.S. reserve units into active duty, and Khrushchev backed down. In mid-1963, Kennedy went to West Berlin and made friends of all the citizens in a stirring speech that ended "*Ich bin ein Berliner*"—translated as "I am a Berliner." The intricate inflections of the German language provide an amusing anecdote about that speech. What Kennedy should have said was, "Ich bin Berliner." Instead, he actually told the West German crowd that he was a jelly doughnut.

There was trouble over Cuba once again in late 1962 when U.S. intelligence discovered that the Russians were building nuclear missile bases on the island. The missiles could have reached about two-thirds of the eastern United States. Kennedy announced a U.S. blockade. He declared that the United States would turn back any ships bound for Cuba from anywhere if they were found to carry offensive weapons. He also told Khrushchev that an attack on the United States from Cuba would be regarded as an attack from the Soviet Union. The world held its collective breath. Would the Russians send a ship to Cuba? Would the U.S. blockade stop it? What then? Was this war? Finally, Khrushchev answered the President. He would dismantle the missiles if the United States agreed not to invade Cuba. It was done, and the world breathed a bit easier.

Another trouble spot, about which Americans knew little but would learn much, was in Southeast Asia. There was ongoing friction and fighting between Communist North Vietnam and U.S.-backed South Vietnam. By the time Kennedy took office, some 1,000 U.S. military advisers were in South Vietnam.

Although Kennedy would not commit U.S. fighting forces to the region, he did authorize more advisers, and they numbered some 16,000 by his death. It is impossible to know what would have happened in that region had Kennedy lived, but U.S. involvement escalated over the next years and resulted in the tragic and divisive Vietnam War.

Things were not exactly calm at home either. The fight for civil rights, brought ever more into the public conscience by the

Martin Luther King, Jr., waves to the crowd after delivering his "I have a dream" speech in Washington, D.C., on August 28, 1963.

Supreme Court decision of 1954, was gathering momentum. James Meredith, an African American, tried to enroll at the all-white University of Mississippi. Alabama's Governor George Wallace stood in the door of the state university to keep blacks out. The Reverend Martin Luther King, Jr., began his protest marches in Birmingham, Alabama. Riots and fights broke out in the streets. Marchers and protesters were led off to jail. Kennedy had never been a strong civil rights advocate during his years in Congress. During his campaign and into his presidency, he had never made civil rights or women's issues a top priority. Now, however, he sensed the time had come. He called for freedom and justice for all Americans. On television, he challenged Americans to be fair in their dealings with others and he asked his brother Bobby, now attorney general, to intervene in voting rights cases in the South. On television in June 1963, he promised to have important civil rights legislation enacted. He did, in fact, send a strong civil rights bill to Congress. However, its passage was delayed and in the meantime, Kennedy was assassinated. As a result, no civil rights legislation was passed during the Kennedy years.

But there were successes. The Peace Corps was established in 1961 and became very popular with Americans of all ages as the President challenged them to help developing countries. The number of Americans who responded reached a record high in 1966 with more than 15,000 members in 52 countries. Based on individual skills, volunteers are assigned to specific projects in certain countries and are expected to remain for two years, speaking the language, living at the same level as the people they help, and aiding in development. The Peace Corps is still serving abroad today with some 5,000 volunteers in about 90 countries.

Building on a Good Neighbor policy, Kennedy established the Alliance for Progress in 1961. It provides U.S. dollars for Latin American aid.

In May 1961, Alan Shepard became the first American in space, and Kennedy announced the country's intention of placing a man on the moon by the end of the decade. The following February, John Glenn, later a U.S. senator from Ohio, became the first American in orbit. In July of that year, Kennedy signed a nuclear test ban treaty with the Soviet Union and Great Britain.

Nearing the end of 1963, the country was responding to the Kennedy mystique. Jacqueline was beautifying the White House and turning it into an even more cultured showplace of American life. Bright young people were flooding to Washington to offer their ideas and energies to get the country moving. The drive for civil rights was on the march. College campuses were alive with ideas and energies for making the tired old world a better place. The Kennedy children were scampering about the Oval Office or the White House lawn. Kennedy himself seemed to be everywhere, laughing, energetic, full of vitality and hope.

And then it all fell apart in Dallas, Texas. Jack Kennedy was nothing if not an astute politician. He was well aware of his popularity with the people. He was also well aware that he had entered the White House on a frighteningly slim margin. Thinking he would face Republican conservative Barry Goldwater in the 1964 election, he felt he had to strengthen his political support now. One of the problem areas was Texas, home state of Vice President Johnson. With its 32 electoral votes for President, Texas was an important prize. But state Governor John Connally and Senator Ralph Yarborough were feuding over several issues. Kennedy decided to go to Dallas and tour the state with both men as a show of unity.

On November 22, 1963, Jack and Jackie Kennedy rode in the rear of an open limousine with Governor and Mrs. Connally in the seats directly in front of them. The crowds along the route of the motorcade were friendly and cheering. At one point, Mrs. Connally turned back to Kennedy and said, "Mr. President, you can't say Dallas doesn't love you."

A few moments later, at 12:30 P.M. Central Time, the President's car passed the Texas School Book Depository. Shots rang out. It is doubtful that Kennedy ever knew what happened. One shot tore through his neck. The second removed the back of his head on the right side. Governor Connally was severely wounded as well.

The President was rushed to Parkland Hospital where he was pronounced dead shortly after 1 P.M. There was never any hope of recovery. A stunned and horrified nation sat before television sets for the next few days. Lee Harvey Oswald, a 24-year-old citizen of Dallas, was charged with the assassination. While being led through police quarters in front of television cameras on Sunday evening, November 24, he was killed by nightclub owner Jack Ruby, also of Dallas.

John (John-John) F. Kennedy, Jr., directly in front of the President's brother Robert, salutes as the casket containing the body of his father leaves St. Matthew's Cathedral in Washington, D.C., on November 25, 1963. Caroline, the President's daughter, stands in front of Edward Kennedy, alongside her mother, Jacqueline Kennedy.

It was a bizarre and terrible time. Questions swirled about why and how this could happen. The Warren Commission, set up to investigate, concluded that Oswald, who had once lived in the Soviet Union, had acted alone. Others felt the assassination was a conspiracy led by Cuba's Castro or organized crime figures, but there has never been any conclusive proof of that. Even though some still hold lingering doubts, most Americans accept the findings of the Warren Commission.

John Fitzgerald Kennedy, thirty-fifth President of the United States, was buried in Arlington Cemetery where an "eternal flame" marks his grave. Perhaps the most lasting impressions of those terrible days following his death were those of the First Lady. She held the wounded head of her husband as he lay dying. She stood in the President's plane, *Air Force One*, her pink suit still bloodied, as Lyndon B. Johnson became the thirty-sixth President of the United States. With quiet dignity, she held the hands of her children as they watched their father's funeral procession. Shrouded in black, she carried the grief of the nation as well as her own with composure and silent sorrow.

The country never forgot Jacqueline Kennedy. She raised her children quietly, moving from the White House to Georgetown, a suburb of Washington, D.C. In 1964, she moved to New York City and four years later married Greek shipping tycoon Aristotle Onassis. After his death, she continued to live in New York City where she worked as a book editor. She died of cancer in 1995, a First Lady second only perhaps to Eleanor Roosevelt in the love and admiration of the public and a woman who had become a legend in her own time. She is buried next to the President in Arlington Cemetery. Caroline Kennedy, a lawyer, married designer Edwin Schlossberg in 1987. John F. Kennedy, Jr., a lawyer and magazine editor, married Carolyn Bessette in 1996 and lives in New York City.

John F. Kennedy was the fourth President of the United States to be assassinated. His time in the Oval Office was far too short to know if he could have become the leader of his promise. That he inspired the country, especially its young people, there is no doubt. Kennedy's death changed the nation perhaps even more than his life in the White House could have done. For a short time, anything seemed possible and worth fighting for. Perhaps it was only Camelot, but it was real all the same. The lasting tragedy is that we will never know what might have been.

Names in the News in Kennedy's Time

Helen Keller (1880–1968):

Blind and deaf U.S. author who did much to further education of the disabled. Taught by Anne Sullivan. Their story was depicted in the 1959 Pulitzer Prize-winning play *The Miracle Worker*, and in the 1962 film of the same name.

Robert F. Kennedy (1925–1968):

Brother of the President; conducted JFK's presidential campaign; attorney general during his brother's administration. He was assassinated while campaigning for presidential nomination (1968).

Martin Luther King, Jr. (1929–1968):

Georgia-born Baptist minister; led mass civil rights movement from mid-1950s. His nonviolent philosophy challenged white American conscience, and brought political pressure for civil rights legislation. Famous for "I have a dream" speech at 1963 March on Washington. Assassinated in Memphis, Tennessee.

Chapter Five

L.B.J. and a Time for Civil Rights

Lyndon B. Johnson (1963-1969)

It was a history lesson on government in action that no one wanted to see. But it was a history lesson that those who watched never forgot. The hour was 2:39 P.M. Central Time. The place was the cabin of *Air Force One*, the President's plane, sitting on the tarmac of Love Field in Dallas, Texas. Jacqueline Kennedy, her clothes splattered with the blood of her just assassinated husband, stood quietly. Claudia "Lady Bird" Johnson held the Bible as U.S. District Court Judge Sarah T. Hughes administered the oath of office to a solemn Lyndon Baines Johnson, now thirty-sixth President of the United States.

John F. Kennedy had been pronounced dead less than two hours earlier. He had been assassinated in a horrifying tragedy witnessed by thousands on television. The governor of Texas was wounded and perhaps near death as well. No one was certain what had happened or why. Fear and chaos rocked the Texas city and the nation. Yet, in the cabin of *Air Force One*, the U.S. Constitution was quietly at work as the reins of power passed on. Fate and an assassin's bullet had put Lyndon Johnson in the White House.

Actually, Johnson had had his eye on the White House for a long time. He came by an interest in politics naturally. A grandfather, Joseph W. Baines, had been the Texas secretary of state in the mid-1800s. His father, Sam Ealy Johnson, Jr., was a farmer and a member of the Texas House of Representatives. His mother,

Rebekah Baines Johnson, edited a small, local newspaper.

Born near Stonewall, Texas, on August 27, 1908, Lyndon, the oldest of five children, was known as Baby for three months because his parents couldn't decide what to call him. They finally chose the name of a family friend. When he was five years old, his family moved to Johnson City, Texas. Times were tough for the Johnson family, but there were fun times, too. Lyndon grew into a crack marble shooter, and he remembered the most exciting day of his boyhood as a visit to the Alamo with his father. He was thrilled with the bravery of Davy Crockett and others who defended the mission against the invaders from Mexico.

Johnson, who would grow to be six feet three, was a lanky boy who took dancing lessons and studied the violin for a time. He was bright, hated math, and often misbehaved in class. He did win debating honors, however, at Johnson City High School. After graduation in 1924, his mother urged him to go to college, but he took off for California with some friends in a used Model-T Ford. Several months later, he was back in Texas flat broke. Eventually, he found his way to Southwest Texas State Teachers College, from which he graduated in 1930.

Four years later he met and married Claudia Alta Taylor, known as Lady Bird. She had graduated near the top of her class from the University of Texas. Lyndon asked Lady Bird for a date the first time he met her, but she refused. Undaunted, he kept telephoning her. Finally, she agreed to go out with him. When he proposed marriage she accepted. They were wed in November 1934, in San Antonio.

Senate Majority Leader Lyndon Johnson of Texas and his wife, Lady Bird, at Bethesda Naval Hospital in July 1955, where he was recuperating from a heart attack.

After a honeymoon in Mexico, they hurried on to Washington, D.C., where Lyndon was secretary to a congressman.

The Johnsons had two daughters, Lynda Bird and Luci Baines. Lady Bird became a much admired First Lady, especially for her beautification of America program. She advocated passage of the Highway Beautification Act of 1965, which restricted billboards and junkyards along the nation's superhighways.

Johnson won a seat in the House of Representatives in 1937 and stayed there for another six terms. He was befriended by the powerful speaker of the House, Sam Rayburn—also from Texas—which did not hurt his career any. He took time out from politics for active duty with the navy during World War II. He was a lieutenant commander serving in Australia and New Guinea and won a Silver Star after his observation plane survived an attack by Japanese aircraft.

In 1949, Johnson made it to the Senate. He rose in power, chairing such committees as the Senate Aeronautics and Space Sciences, and became the Democratic minority leader in 1953. The Democrats gained control of the Senate the following year, making Johnson, at age 45, the youngest majority leader in Senate history. Lyndon Johnson was perhaps without parallel in leadership of the Senate, possessing an extraordinary managerial skill that he also brought to the White House. Critics often ridiculed what they called his blunt Texas mannerisms. He was labeled ruthless and driven, a complex, ambitious man, a master manipulator who loved power. If so, he was also a political genius. President Richard Nixon said LBJ was "one of the ablest political craftsmen of our times."

Interestingly enough, it was the election of Dwight Eisenhower, a Republican, as President in 1952 that really boosted Johnson's career. During the Eisenhower years, Johnson displayed his skill as a negotiator and was able to produce a remarkably disciplined Congress to work with the opposition President. As majority leader, Democrat Johnson promised not to oppose

Eisenhower just for the sake of opposition. "All of us," he said, reflecting a sentiment rarely heard in the late twentieth century, "are Americans before we are members of any political organization."

However, Johnson's career as majority leader suffered a setback soon after it started. A moderately severe heart attack in the summer of 1955 took him away from his beloved Senate, but he was back in six months. His skilled leadership played a major role in the passage of the civil rights bills of 1957 and 1960, which protected voting rights. His leadership seems all the more remarkable since, until 1957, Johnson had always voted with his southern colleagues against civil rights legislation. LBJ emerged from the Eisenhower years as a national figure rather than only a political leader from the South.

By the time of the 1960 Democratic presidential convention, Johnson was a leading candidate, but he lost out to John Kennedy on the first ballot. Then, to almost everyone's surprise, Kennedy picked Johnson as his running mate. An even bigger surprise, he accepted! Why did he trade the great power of Senate majority leader for the relatively boring—and relatively powerless—vice president's job? No one really knew, except perhaps Johnson himself, although political experts generally agree that the Democrats would not have won the election without Johnson's ability to carry the states of Texas, Louisiana, and the Carolinas.

For a man who relished the use of power, LBJ was bored being vice president. About the only satisfaction he found was as chairman of the National Aeronautics and Space Council and the President's Committee on Equal Employment Opportunity. Although he personally got along well with Kennedy, he never could see eye to eye with the young eastern liberals who dominated the President's staff.

But they say that being vice president is only a heartbeat away from the ultimate power. In Johnson's case, he was two cars away on November 22, 1963, when Jack Kennedy was

On November 22, 1963, Vice President Lyndon B. Johnson, flanked by his wife, Lady Bird (left), and Jacqueline Kennedy, is sworn in as President of the U.S. aboard Air Force One, the presidential plane, in Dallas, Texas, following Kennedy's assassination.

assassinated in Dallas, Texas. Two hours later, Lyndon Baines Johnson was the thirty-sixth President of the United States.

Said a solemn President to Congress a few days later, "All I have, I would have given gladly not to be standing here today." He pledged to continue Kennedy's programs. Kennedy's dream, said the new President, would not die. Then, this lifelong son of the South urged Congress to pass a pending civil rights bill.

The country was in great turmoil following Kennedy's assassination, and Johnson is credited with calming the public and serving as the symbol of continuing stability in government. Although he was often compared unfavorably with the sophisticated Kennedy, LBJ was able—through skill and leadership—to get Congress to pass impressive and long overdue legislation concerning civil rights, conservation, and antipoverty measures.

Lyndon Johnson was elected President in his own right in November 1964, with Hubert H. Humphrey of Minnesota as his running mate. LBJ interpreted his popular majority of more than 15 million votes over Republican conservative Barry Goldwater as a stamp of approval for his Great Society program. The Great Society called for civil rights legislation, the medical health programs of Medicare and Medicaid, environmental protection laws, and a war on poverty.

During the next few years, the most turbulent in U.S. political history, President Johnson, often following what had been Kennedy's plan, was able to pass a lot of legislation through the

Democratic Congress. His War on Poverty created the Office of Economic Opportunity, with its Job Corps to provide vocational training, a domestic Peace Corps to aid the nation's ghettos, and a Head Start program for disadvantaged preschoolers. Through the Social Security system, Medicare provided hospital insurance for those 65 years and older, and Medicaid gave hospital and medical benefits to the poor of any age. The Water Quality Act of 1965 prompted states to set up water quality standards, and the Clear Air Act set auto emission standards. Consumers benefited from the Fair Packaging and Labeling Act of 1966, which required contents to be listed on labels.

However, Johnson's policies were not all popular nor all successful. The War on Poverty was generally a failure, his leadership led to rising hostilities in Vietnam, and his liberal attitudes brought on a conservative backlash that allowed the Republicans to return to the White House after the next election.

In 1967, President Johnson appointed Thurgood Marshall to the Supreme Court. Marshall became the first African American to sit on the nation's highest court. But the crowning glory of the Johnson administration was its civil rights legislation. The Civil Rights Act of 1964 barred discrimination in hotels, restaurants, and other public facilties, and in employment in general. The Voting Rights Act of 1965, the President's proudest achievement, outlawed the unfairly used literacy tests that had often kept blacks out of the voting booth. The Civil Rights Act of 1968 barred discrimination in the sale and rental of housing.

President Johnson turns to shake Reverend Martin Luther King, Jr.'s, hand and to give him the pen after signing the Civil Rights Act of 1964.

The result of all this legislation was a dramatic increase in minority voting registration and some of the most shocking violence in American history. As African American leaders such as Martin Luther King, Jr., urged nonviolence, more militant black groups spoke out against the white establishment. But white supremacists and even those who had heretofore considered themselves "moderate" on the question of race were not going to go down easy.

From 1964 to 1968, cities all across the United States seemed awash in rioting. There were riots in more than 100 American cities during 1967 alone, with 100 dead and thousands injured and arrested. In the North, Detroit, Michigan, suffered through five days of rioting. In the South, King led a peaceful march from Selma, Alabama, to Montgomery in early 1965. But shortly after the march, a nighttime lynch party shot to death a white volunteer worker, Mrs. Viola Gregg Liuzzo from Detroit, for her part in the protest. Bull Connor, the police chief of Birmingham, Alabama, let his dogs loose on a group of peaceful marchers. Connor's backers shouted racial slurs as the marchers ran in fear. Here and there throughout the South, black college students, sometimes joined by whites, quietly sat at segregated lunch counters. Thus began the "sit-ins" that spread throughout the country. For the most part they were nonviolent and peaceful, but basically this was a nation in painful torment.

Interestingly, the growing ferment over civil rights neatly paralleled the beginning of a new women's rights movement, as U.S. women began to look at the inequality in their own lives. Soon the cry would begin for equal pay for women in the workplace, for equal access to higher education and to sports scholarships, for abortion rights and child care, and for an equal entrance into the political arena. This new thrust was captured in one of the bumper stickers of the time: "A women's place is in the House...and in the Senate." And just maybe in the White House as well.

On March 31, 1968, in the midst of all this turmoil, Lyndon Johnson further startled the nation by announcing that he would not seek another term. Why? The answer may well be traced to far-off Southeast Asia and the tortured country of Vietnam.

After World War II, France began fighting Communist and nationalist forces to regain control of Vietnam, which had been a French colony in the mid-1800s. The French were finally defeated at Dienbienphu on May 8, 1954. Vietnam was divided. The Communists controlled the north with the capital at Hanoi, and the nationalists were in South Vietnam with its capital at Saigon. The two sides had been fighting for years. The United States, afraid that the fall of South Vietnam would open Southeast Asia to Communist domination, was slowly drawn into the conflict. At first, only American "advisers" were sent to the region, a practice escalated by Kennedy. But in August 1964, North Vietnam attacked the U.S. destroyer *Maddox* in the Gulf of Tonkin. The United States fired back with air strikes, and a few days later President Johnson asked for, and got, authority from Congress to take "all necessary measures" against further attacks. It was not a formal declaration of war, but it allowed the President to act as though war was being conducted. When 3,500 U.S. Marines were sent to South Vietnam in March 1965, it marked the beginning of eight years of American participation in the war in that country.

As though Vietnam were not enough, Johnson faced a new challenge in 1967 when Israel was victorious over Egypt in the so-called Six-Day War. The Soviet Union demanded that the United Nations condemn Israel. Johnson

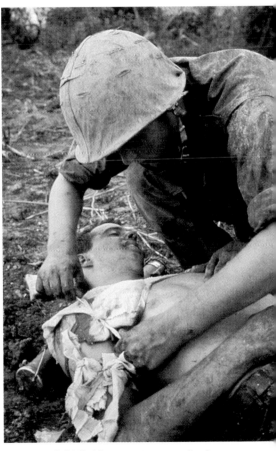

A U.S. Marine gives medical attention to a wounded soldier in June 1967 during the conflict in South Vietnam.

kept the United States neutral. A summit conference in New Jersey, between Johnson and the Soviet leader, Aleksei Kosygin, did not change either country's positions on the Middle East or Vietnam, but the U.S. President emerged from the talks with a new statesmanlike image for his restraint and reasonableness.

The war in Vietnam would not end until 1975, with a Communist victory. The country would be unified a year later. But until then, it was the United States that was nearly torn apart.

By 1968, 550,000 Americans were fighting in Vietnam. By the cease-fire, more than 50,000 Americans would die. More and more, the country was split. The Hawks, fearful of Communist takeover in the region, called for more and more involvement. The Doves wanted negotiations at once. The growing counterculture made itself known as cries of "No! No! I won't go!" came from young men as they burned their draft cards or escaped to Canada to avoid service. Demonstrators marched on the Pentagon; college campuses erupted with protests. Americans were increasingly shocked by the sight of Buddhist monks setting themselves on fire in Vietnam in war protest and by the account of the My Lai massacre when an American army officer was accused of murdering Vietnamese civilians.

The rift in the country was horrendous. Demonstrators went so far as to stand on the White House lawn chanting "LBJ, LBJ, How many kids did you kill today?" The gap between the President's assurances of seeking peace and the ongoing war casualties was too great. Sensing that he could not win and perhaps unwilling to endure the fractious campaign that would surely emerge, Lyndon Johnson announced on March 31, 1968 that he would not run for reelection.

Just four days later, on April 4, 1968, civil rights leader Martin Luther King, Jr., was assassinated as he stood on a balcony in Memphis, Tennessee. This triggered one of the last riots of the sixties. His assassin, James Earl Ray, is still in jail. Two months later, Bobby Kennedy, brother of the slain President and himself expected to run in the next election, was assassinated in Los Angeles by a resident alien, Sirhan Sirhan, also still in jail.

The outgoing President did not attend the 1968 convention, which nominated Hubert Humphrey, who would lose to Richard Nixon that November. After the new President was sworn in on January 20, 1969, Lyndon and Lady Bird Johnson went home to their ranch near Johnson City, Texas. He tended his land, gave some public speeches, and wrote his memoirs. LBJ survived a second heart attack in 1972 but died of a third attack on January 22, 1973, less than a week before the end of the war in Vietnam. He is buried in the family plot near Johnson City.

Lyndon Baines Johnson, the tall man from Texas with the craggy face and big ears, led the nation through its most turbulent domestic era. His critics fault his handling of U.S. involvement in Vietnam. His admirers point to the aims and accomplishments of the Great Society. Many praise his remarkable leadership of Congress and the civil rights legislation that was passed during his years in the White House. In all this, LBJ was surely, as presidential hopeful Adlai Stevenson once said, "a master of the art of the possible in politics." James A. Farley had a simpler, more direct message. Said the chairman of the Democratic National Committee, "We never had a finer leader."

Prior to his retirement to the ranch in Johnson City, Texas, in 1969, President Johnson demonstrates his cattle herding techniques by "cutting" out a cow from the herd during a press barbeque in November 1964.

Names in the News in Johnson's Time

Barry M. Goldwater (1909–):

Arizona conservative senator, defeated by Johnson in 1964 campaign.

Hubert H. Humphrey (1911–1978):

Liberal senator from Minnesota (1949–1965, 1971–1978); vice president under LBJ; defeated by Nixon in 1968 presidential campaign.

Willie Mays (1931–):

One of baseball's greatest (NY/SF Giants, NY Mets); the "Say Hey Kid" Hall of Famer (1979).

William Westmoreland (1914–):

Army general, appointed by Johnson to command U.S. forces in Vietnam (1964–1968); army chief of staff (1968–1972).

The United States in 1959

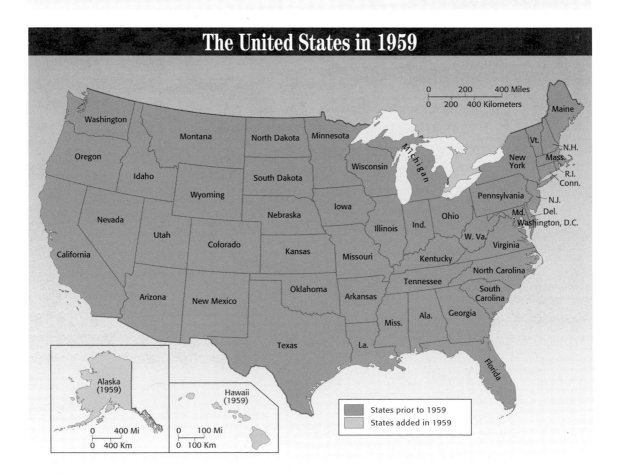

The last two states, Alaska and Hawaii, added in 1959, have brought the United States to its present size.

32. Franklin Delano Roosevelt (1933–1945)

Democratic party; age at inauguration, 51
Born: Hyde Park, New York, January 30, 1882
Died: Warm Springs, Georgia, April 12, 1945
Education; occupation: Harvard; lawyer
Family: Anna Eleanor Roosevelt (married 1905);
   children: Anna Eleanor, James, Elliott, Franklin Delano, Jr., John
Important events during Roosevelt's terms:
    1933: New Deal measures enacted;
        Twenty-First Amendment passed to repeal Prohibition.
    1934: Securities and Exchange Commission (SEC) created.
    1935: Work Projects Administration (WPA), Social Security Act
    1939: World War II begins with German invasion of Poland.
    1941: Japan attacks Pearl Harbor, U.S. enters war.
    1942: Marines invade Guadalcanal, Allies invade North Africa;
        Office of Price Administration created.
    1943: Allies invade Italy; Cairo and Teheran conferences
    1944: D-Day, Allies invade Europe.
    1945: Yalta Conference

33. Harry S Truman (1945–1953)

Democratic party; age at inauguration, 60
Born: Lamar, Missouri, May 8, 1884
Died: Kansas City, Missouri, December 26, 1972
Education; occupation: Kansas City Law School; politician
Family: Elizabeth Wallace (married 1919); children: Margaret
Important events during Truman's terms:
    1945: San Francisco conference; end of WWII in Europe;
        dropping of atom bombs; Japanese surrender; UN charter signed.
    1946: Atomic Energy Commission created; Truman Doctrine announced.
    1947: Taft-Hartley Act passed.
    1948: Marshall Plan to aid European recovery

1950: Korean War begins.

1951: Truman relieves MacArthur of command; Twenty-Second Amendment ratified.

34. Dwight David Eisenhower (1953–1961)

Republican party; age at inauguration, 62

Born: Denison, Texas, October 14, 1890

Died: Washington, D.C., March 28, 1969

Education; occupation: West Point; soldier

Family: Mamie Geneva Doud (married 1916);

  children: Doud Dwight, John Sheldon

Important events during Eisenhower's terms:

    1953: Department of Health, Education, and Welfare created; Korean War armistice signed.

    1954: First atomic submarine *Nautilus* launched.

    1957: Eisenhower Doctrine announced; Civil Rights Commission created; Soviets launch *Sputnik*.

    1958: First U.S. satellite—*Explorer I*—in orbit.

    1959: Alaska, Hawaii admitted as 49th and 50th states; St. Lawrence Seaway opens.

35. John Fitzgerald Kennedy (1961–1963)

Democratic party; age at inauguration, 43

Born: Brookline, Massachusetts, May 29, 1917

Died: Dallas, Texas, November 22, 1963

Education, occupation: Harvard; politician

Family: Jacqueline Lee Bouvier (married 1953);

  children: Caroline, John, Patrick

Important events during Kennedy's term:

    1961: Peace Corps created; first man in space (Soviet's Yuri Gargarin); Bay of Pigs invasion; first American in space (Alan Shepard); Berlin Wall built.

    1962: First American in orbit (John Glenn); U.S. troops sent to Vietnam; Cuban missile crisis

36. Lyndon Baines Johnson (1963–1969)

Democratic party; age at inauguration, 55

Born: Stonewall, Texas, August 17, 1908

Died: San Antonio, Texas, January 22, 1973

Education, occupation: Southwest Texas State Teachers College; politician

Family: Claudia Taylor (married 1934);
   children: Lynda Bird, Luci Baines

Important events during Johnson's terms:

   1964: Civil Rights Act passed.

   1965: Voting Rights Act passed;
            Housing and Urban Development department created;
            Medicare established; fighting in Vietnam escalates.

   1966: Department of Transportation created.

   1967: Arab-Israeli war

   1968: Tet offensive in Vietnam;
            Martin Luther King, Jr., Robert Kennedy assassinated.

Glossary

airlift System of transporting people and cargo by plane usually into an area inaccessible by other means.

Atomic Age Name given to the period following the dropping of first atomic bomb on Japan signaling the end of World War II in the Pacific.

beatnik A person who rejects the ways of established society in dress and/or behavior; term used mainly in 1960s.

blacklist A list of persons who are disapproved of and boycotted, such as those suspected by Senator Joseph McCarthy of being Communists in the 1950s.

breadline A line of people waiting to receive free food, usually during a depression.

Cold War Period of conflict without military intervention, generally applied to relations between the U.S.S.R. and the U.S. after World War II.

Communist One who follows the theory of communism, a system of government based on an all-powerful single-party state and the abolition of private property.

counterculture A culture whose values run opposite to those of the established society.

counteroffensive A large-scale military operation taken by a force previously on the defensive.

D-Day Denotes the first day of any military operation. Most famous D-Day took place on June 6, 1944, when the Allies landed on the coast of France and signaled the end of Nazi domination of Europe in World War II.

depression In government, a period of low general economic activity.

domino theory The belief that if one nation becomes Communist-controlled, neighboring nations will do likewise.

Dove In government, an opponent of war.

egghead An intellectual highbrow, used as a derogatory term in the 1950s.

five-star general Highest U.S. army rank, created 1944.

Hawk In government, one who advocates war.

insubordination Act of disobeying authority, as in the military.

kamikaze Japanese word meaning "divine wind." Denoted Japanese pilots during World War II who deliberately crashed their planes, usually onto U.S. ships in the Pacific.

New Deal Franklin Roosevelt's program of economic recovery from the Great Depression.

newsreel In movie theaters, a short film dealing with current events, usually preceding the featured film; generally discontinued in recent times.

pacifist One strongly opposed to conflict, especially war.

pinks Name for light-colored army officer uniform trousers during World War II.

plank In government, an article in the platform of a political party.

polio Full name, poliomyelitis: Infectious viral disease characterized by motor paralysis, now largely erased by the Salk vaccine.

robber baron In late nineteenth century, person who became wealthy by exploiting workers or natural resources

sit-in Organized protest by sitting in the seats or on the floor of an establishment to protest policy, usually of racial discrimination.

Sputnik Russian satellite, first to orbit the Earth, October 4, 1957.

Third Reich (Third Empire) Term for Hitler's Nazi government.

whistle-stop campaign Political campaign trip that makes many stops in small communities, originally from the rear platform of a train.

witch hunt Deliberate harassment, generally of political opponents.

Further Reading

Anderson, Catherine C. *Jacqueline Kennedy Onassis: Woman of Courage*. Lerner, 1995

Beyer, Don E. *The Manhattan Project: America Makes the First Atomic Bomb*. Franklin Watts, 1991

Eskow, Dennis. *Lyndon Baines Johnson*. Franklin Watts, 1993

Ferrell, Robert H. *Harry S. Truman and the Bomb*. High Plains, 1996

Hills, Ken. *1960s*, "Take Ten Years" series. Raintree Steck-Vaughn, 1992

Kort, Michael G. *Cold War*. Millbrook Press, 1994

Larsen, Rebecca. *Franklin D. Roosevelt: Man of Destiny*. Franklin Watts, 1991.

Mayo, Edith, ed. *The Smithsonian Book of the First Ladies: Their Lives, Times, and Issues*. Holt, 1996

Mills, Judie. *John F. Kennedy*. Franklin Watts, 1988

Morris, Jeffrey. *The Truman Way*, "Great Presidential Decisions" series. Lerner, 1994

Moskin, J. Robert. *Mr. Truman's War*. Random House, 1996

Netzley, Patricia D. *The Assassination of President John F. Kennedy*. Silver Burdett Press, 1994

Patterson, Charles. *The Civil Rights Movement*. Facts on File, 1995

Powledge, Fred. *We Shall Overcome: Heroes of the Civil Rights Movement*. Simon & Schuster, 1993

Ross, Stewart. *World War II*, "Causes and Consequences" series. Raintree Steck-Vaughn, 1995

Schraff, Anne E. *Great Depression and the New Deal: America's Economic Collapse and Recovery*. Franklin Watts, 1990

Schuman, Michael A. *Eleanor Roosevelt: First Lady and Humanitarian*. Enslow, 1995

Stewart, Gail B. *New Deal*. Macmillan Children's, 1993

Wormser, Richard L. *Growing Up in the Great Depression*. Atheneum, 1994

Wright, David. *Vietnam War*, "Causes and Consequences" series. Raintree Steck-Vaughn, 1995

Index